Wilderness, Morality, and Value

Wilderness, Morality, and Value

Joshua S. Duclos

LEXINGTON BOOKS
Lanham • Boulder • New York • London

Published by Lexington Books
An imprint of The Rowman & Littlefield Publishing Group, Inc.
4501 Forbes Boulevard, Suite 200, Lanham, Maryland 20706
www.rowman.com

86-90 Paul Street, London EC2A 4NE

Copyright © 2022 by The Rowman & Littlefield Publishing Group, Inc.

All rights reserved. No part of this book may be reproduced in any form or by any electronic or mechanical means, including information storage and retrieval systems, without written permission from the publisher, except by a reviewer who may quote passages in a review.

British Library Cataloguing in Publication Information Available

Library of Congress Cataloging-in-Publication Data

Names: Duclos, Joshua S., author.
  Title: Wilderness, morality, and value / Joshua S. Duclos.
  Description: Lanham : Lexington Books, an imprint of The Rowman & Littlefield Publishing Group, Inc., [2022] | Includes bibliographical references and index. | Summary: "The pursuit of wilderness preservation is at odds with a commitment to animal welfare. Wilderness, Morality, and Value charts a way forward by clarifying the meaning of wilderness, investigating the fundamental value of wilderness itself, and exploring the implications of a religio-spiritual valuation of wilderness"-- Provided by publisher.
  Identifiers: LCCN 2022023547 (print) | LCCN 2022023548 (ebook) | ISBN 9781666901368 (cloth) | ISBN 9781666901382 (paperback) | ISBN9781666901375 (epub)
  Subjects: LCSH: Nature conservation--Moral and ethical aspects. | Wildlife conservation--Moral and ethical aspects. | Animal welfare--Moral and ethical aspects. | Wilderness areas--Management.
  Classification: LCC QH75 .D825 2022 (print) | LCC QH75 (ebook) | DDC 333.95/16--dc23/eng/20220615
  LC record available at https://lccn.loc.gov/2022023547
  LC ebook record available at https://lccn.loc.gov/2022023548

Contents

Acknowledgments	vii
Introduction	ix
Chapter One: Uncomplicating the Idea of Wilderness	1
Chapter Two: The Moral Ambiguity of Wilderness Preservation	23
Chapter Three: Intrinsic Value and Nonanthropocentrism	45
Chapter Four: Value and Wilderness *qua* Wilderness	75
Chapter Five: To Be or Not to Be Prometheus	97
Bibliography	127
Index	135
About the Author	141

Acknowledgments

Creating this book required the support of many institutions and individuals. I am especially indebted to the faculty and staff of the Frederick S. Pardee Center for the Study of the Longer-Range Future. The Pardee Center took me on as a summer fellow in 2016 and afforded me an opportunity for concentrated research and writing. They also facilitated close conversation with biologists, economists, and environmental scientists whose work challenged and informed my own. My sincere gratitude to the late Anthony Janetos, former Director of the Pardee Center, and to Ms. Cynthia Barakatt, former Associate Director, for fostering a vibrant culture of interdisciplinary inquiry.

Several scholars at Boston University deserve special thanks, most notably Daniel Dahlstrom. Dan read and commented on the entire manuscript. His capacious, charitable intellect led to innumerable improvements. David Roochnik's philosophical conversation, wit, and friendship were invaluable during long years of thinking and writing. Walter Hopp and Charles Griswold were inspiring interlocutors; they also exemplified how one goes about being a dedicated scholar as well as a first-rate teacher.

My early teachers at Connecticut College had their part to play, as well. Thank you to Bruce Kirmmse, Derek Turner, Larry Vogel, and Mel Woody for kindling a love of wisdom, and for holding my feet to the fire when I attempted to turn in shoddy work. Their lessons have not been forgotten: *Tanquam lignum quod plantatum est secus decursus aquarium*. From the University of Chicago, I must thank Gabrielle Richardson Lear and Leon Kass. Their writing and teaching helped me think about virtue, goodness, and ethics in new, fruitful ways.

St. Paul's School in Concord, New Hampshire generously provided financial support during the summer of 2021. This support permitted me to take a break from summer teaching and devote myself to revising the manuscript. Many colleagues at St. Paul's provided equally important moral support as I brough this book to completion.

Working through the problems of philosophy can be lonely, heavy work. Several friends ameliorated the loneliness and lightened the load. Brendan Bucy joined me on countless runs around Boston. On these runs, we experimented with ideas on everything from wilderness to free will to Periclean statecraft. A few of the arguments in this book began as breathless attempts to explain a point as we fought through cramped legs on the last stretch of Commonwealth Avenue. Cameron Hewitt was a thoughtful and thought-provoking companion during sojourns in the mountains. Elizabeth Duclos-Orsello was ready with a sympathetic ear when the work was going poorly; she was equally ready to celebrate with a Negroni when the work was going well.

For seeing the book's potential and bringing it to press, I would like to thank Jana Hodges-Kluck and her team at Rowman & Littlefield. They were generous with their time and patient when fielding my many questions.

The first chapter of this book first appeared in unrevised form as "Uncomplicating the Idea of Wilderness," *Environmental Values*, volume 29(1), 2020: 89–107, and part of chapter 5 was initially published as "Religious Reasons in the Public Sphere: A Challenge to Habermas," *Philosophy & Theology*, volume 31(1&2), 2020: 121–43. I offer my thanks to Tom Greaves, editor of *Environmental Values*, and James South, editor of *Philosophy & Theology*, for granting permission to reprint this work.

Finally, I thank my mother Elaine and my father Marcel.

Introduction

We have reached a point in history when the continued existence of wilderness cannot be taken for granted. If, two hundred years from now, wilderness areas still exist, it will be because humanity has made a deliberate choice. The idea is disquieting but not hubristic. Left unchecked, humanity now possesses the capacity to hunt, mine, fish, farm, cultivate, settle, augment, destroy or otherwise extend our influence over the entire biosphere. For wilderness to exist into the future, we must decide that it should and then maintain policies to ensure that it does. The decisions and policies will be influenced by the cogency of the arguments given in defense of wilderness. Philosophical analysis of those arguments—particularly the value of, and moral problems associated with, wilderness—has a role to play the future of wilderness itself, whatever that future turns out to be.

Renowned wilderness preservationist Edward Abbey once said that the idea of wilderness needs no defense, only more defenders. But any time a state of affairs ceases to be necessary and instead becomes subject to human volition, it is incumbent upon us to ask normative questions and back up our answers with compelling reasons. In the case of wilderness these questions include: How should the concept of wilderness be understood, and how is it significantly distinct from concepts such as 'nature' and 'environment'? Does wilderness have a unique value *qua* wilderness?[1] Is there a value for which wilderness is a necessary condition? Is the value of wilderness based upon its value to human beings? Or does it possess a value independent of any value it may have for human beings? In other words, is its value anthropocentric, nonanthropocentric, or both, and does it matter? Do we have an obligation to preserve wilderness areas, and if so, why? Or can a case be made, on ethical grounds, for modifying, limiting, or even eliminating wildernesses? The merit of answers to such questions depends upon the merit of the arguments used to support them. Sooner or later, bad arguments come out in the wash. If the ethical foundations of wilderness preservation are shaky, then the entire project is in jeopardy. So I suggest, *pace* Abbey, that wilderness and the idea of wilderness not only need a defense, but that the kind of defense employed matters a great deal.

Since the inception of environmental ethics as a branch of academic philosophy in the late 1960s and early 1970s, there has been a tendency to believe that the best way (perhaps the only way) to safeguard various aspects of the nonhuman natural world is to establish their nonanthropocentric, intrinsic value. It is supposed that doing so will liberate the value (or, alternatively, the meaning, utility, or rights) of the nonhuman natural world from shifting and threatening anthropocentric valuations. In short, if the nonhuman natural world is taken to be valuable in itself and for itself, then perhaps we humans may not be morally permitted to use it, without restriction, for the satisfaction of our own interests. And should the interests of nature conflict with the interests of humanity, it would not be immediately clear that human interests ought to prevail.

A similar line of thought pervades debates about wilderness preservation. There are many anthropocentric reasons to preserve the wilderness, and the more we as humans become convinced that wilderness is of value to us, the more likely it is to be preserved. But the truly moral reasons for wilderness preservation are typically thought to be nonanthropocentric, i.e., reasons that in some sense are grounded in the wilderness's intrinsic value irrespective of its value for human beings. In this book I argue that the ethics of wilderness preservation is seriously complicated by the fact there exists at least one compelling nonanthropocentric reason to oppose wilderness preservation. This reason, which is underrepresented in the philosophical literature and rarely discussed in contemporary environmentalism, generates a moral problem. To appreciate this problem, imagine the following scenario.

There exists, not far from where you live, a mysterious theme park. All year people visit the park to enjoy themselves. The enjoyment takes many forms: thrilling and dangerous rides; peaceful places to relax and rejuvenate; opportunities to create personal meaning and secure spiritual satisfaction; spectacles that delight the senses and kindle wonder; the ability to challenge one's fitness and improve physical health. And like at all theme parks, there are tasty things to eat. The park also serves as a kind of resource center, providing access to material goods, environmental services, and scientific knowledge. The park is mysterious because no one knows who built it, and as far as anyone can tell, no one owns it or operates it. It just exists. Occasionally, though, groups of people come together to provide a measure of management, law, and order.

Then a startling fact comes to light. The operation, indeed, the very existence of the mysterious theme park, entails the enormous and continuous suffering of innumerable sentient organisms. None of the organisms have cognitive capabilities equal to that of a human being, though many are conscious and a few are self-conscious. The creatures are unaware that they are in a park, let alone that the park's existence is predicated on their continued suffering and the condition that they are left there, unaided and unmolested by the millions of human visitors. In the final analysis, the cost of the value that humans derive from the park is the suffering and early death for the millions upon millions of sentient creatures that cause the park to function.

What would be the moral responsibility of an individual or a society upon discovering one of these parks and realizing how it works? Some might say that since the creatures are not human, the moral concern is of relatively small significance. Yet cultures that already recognize the moral—and in some cases legal—standing of animals can hardly be satisfied by such a dismissal. Surely these creatures are owed *something*.

Perhaps one could claim that since the park was not created by humans and is not really sustained by humans (the minimal human management notwithstanding), humans are absolved of moral responsibility. This is a similarly unsatisfying apology. I neither started nor helped sustain the war in Afghanistan, yet it would have been morally repugnant if I had traveled to Kabul to gather resources from and be stimulated, amused, and spiritually or aesthetically gratified by a situation predicated on suffering and early death.

No doubt someone will assert that the park is natural, therefore good, and therefore ought to be left as it is. But such a response is a fallacious appeal to nature. To point out that something is natural is not necessarily to point out that it is good, or desirable, or moral. Admittedly, our moral responsibility in the face of the revelation about the mysterious theme park would be unclear. It would be perfectly clear, however, that we—the users of the park, those who know about its existence—have *some* kind of moral responsibility.

What I want to suggest is that we are already in a situation like the one just described. The mysterious park is the wilderness. Humans did not create the wilderness; its existence does not depend on our own existence. It was here before and could be here after us (though its continued existence may well depend on our desire that it continue to exist). Like the mysterious park, wilderness is a source of enormous value for human beings, including the values of excitement, nourishment, recreation, self-discovery, spirituality, amusement, and aesthetic experience. And just like the mysterious park, the existence of wilderness entails the usually unnoticed suffering and early death of innumerable of sentient beings. Finally, just as human beings would have some kind of moral responsibility in the face of the disturbing revelation about the mysterious theme park, I argue that we have a comparable responsibility in relation to the wilderness. This responsibility entails, at a minimum, that we seriously consider what our moral responsibilities vis-à-vis wilderness actually are. This book is a step in meeting that responsibility.

The general argument of this book is that the wilderness—understood as areas of the earth retaining its primeval character and influence—possesses a distinctive, irreplaceable value for human beings, but that wilderness cannot reasonably be said to possess a nonanthropocentric intrinsic value. Furthermore, because incalculable, ceaseless nonhuman suffering accompanies the distinct anthropocentric value of wilderness, environmental ethics should stop viewing the protection of wilderness as ethically straightforward and start recognizing wilderness as a moral problem. Such a recognition calls for a reexamination of the fundamental nature and a value of wilderness. I take up this task in the following chapters.

Chapter 1 uncomplicates and defends the idea of wilderness stipulated in the 1964 US Wilderness Act. This idea of wilderness has been under attack for three decades, leading some to conclude that it presents intractable philosophical difficulties. I seek to rehabilitate this reasonable and useful understanding of wilderness by presenting and then disarming five persistent criticisms. The idea of wilderness may need a defense, but there is nothing problematic about the idea we have been using, and there is good reason to put recent criticisms aside and keep using it.

Chapter 2 makes the case for the moral ambiguity of wilderness by arguing that, at minimum, we have a nonanthropocentric *pro tanto* moral reason to oppose wilderness preservation.[2] I first demonstrate how and why arguments based on concern for animal welfare are common moral currency among environmentalists when they seek to defend wilderness preservation. Next, I argue that the preservation of wilderness can actually be inimical to animal welfare given the scale and scope of animal suffering the wilderness entails. I formalize an argument called the Objection from Welfare (OFW) and explain how concern for animal welfare can generate a *pro tanto* (albeit counterintuitive) reason to oppose wilderness. I then defend the OFW against four reasonable rebuttals and contend that a fundamental defense of wilderness preservation must generate at least as strong of a moral reason to oppose a limited human augmentation of wilderness as the OFW generates to support it.

Chapter 3 turns to the concepts of nonanthropocentrism and intrinsic value in order to consider the kind of value that could serve as the basis for arguments in defense of wilderness preservation. I argue that there are four kinds of intrinsic value relevant to the wilderness debate, but only one—intrinsic value as ultimate value—can be reasonably ascribed to wilderness, and only then on an anthropocentric basis. I then review the three dominant nonanthropocentric positions in environmental ethics: sentientism, biocentrism, and ecocentrism. I argue that biocentrism and ecocentrism are fatally flawed and that sentientism is the only nonanthropocentric position capable of establishing independent, moral considerability for some parts of the nonhuman natural world. The wilderness is partially comprised of sentient beings, it is not itself sentient; hence, a defense of wilderness grounded in a nonanthropocentric value is unjustifiable. I also argue that the viability of ecocentrism and biocentrism as nonanthropocentric moral positions would have a surprising, unintended influence on debates about wilderness preservation. Should either position turn out to be more plausible than I allow, it would simply strengthen the OFW.

Chapter 4 looks at the extant arguments for wilderness preservation, both anthropocentric and nonanthropocentric. After rejecting for a final time nonanthropocentrism as a basis for a defense of wilderness, I explain the two types of anthropocentric value that have traction in the wilderness debate: instrumental value and ultimate value. While acknowledging that the wide variety of instrumental and ultimate anthropocentric values ascribed to wilderness are currently sufficient for the purposes of environmental activism, I contend that these arguments all share a philosophical shortcoming: they explain that wilderness is a sufficient condition for the satisfaction of a certain value without establishing it as a necessary condition. Moreover, none of the conventional arguments for wilderness preservation focus on the value of wilderness *qua* wilderness. Thought experiments and the reflections of nature writers illustrate that the value of wilderness *qua* wilderness is the value of a worldly domain that is neither created nor controlled by human beings; it is the value of knowing about and being able to experience parts of the earth retaining its primeval characteristics, insignificantly influenced by human activity.

Chapter 4 concludes with scholarship from the Breakthrough Institute. This scholarship suggests that an increasingly artificial, man-managed world is not as fanciful as the thought experiments in chapter 4 make it seem. In addition to illustrating the prospect of world without wilderness, scholarship from the Breakthrough Institute demonstrates the practicality—perhaps even the urgency—of a philosophical consideration of the nature, value, and morality of wilderness preservation.

The fifth and final chapter considers the possibility of rebutting the OFW with an argument grounded in the value of wilderness *qua* wilderness. I begin by drawing a parallel between environmental ethics and bioethics, and then argue that the debate over wilderness preservation can be usefully understood as a debate over what Michael Sandel calls "Promethean aspirations." Sandel argues for human restraint in the field of bioethics by arguing for the moral value of the giftedness of life. I contend Sandel's concept of giftedness in the field of bioethics is analogous to the concept of wilderness in environmental ethics. I then consider the extent to which Sandel's secular argument in defense of giftedness is applicable to a defense of wilderness *qua* wilderness. While Sandel's account makes a significant contribution to our understanding of an anthropocentric valuation of wilderness *qua* wilderness, it fails to generate a moral reason to preserve wilderness that is strong enough to defeat the moral reason to support a limited and pointed augmentation of wilderness per the dictates of the OFW.

I end by demonstrating that the value of wilderness *qua* wilderness—the value of a domain of the other-than-human—can be felicitously interpreted as a religious or spiritual or value. I suggest that one implication of (and perhaps motive for) a spiritual or religious valuation of wilderness is that it permits a sort of teleological suspension of strictly ethical considerations, such that any argument against wilderness, even a moral argument like the OFW, may not be compelling. For those desiring to preserve wilderness, and the distinct value of wilderness *qua* wilderness, at all costs, even in the face of compelling moral arguments to the contrary, a religious or spiritual valuation may be the last redoubt. Such a strategy would, of course, be problematic in a secular liberal democracy. Hence, if I am correct, defenders of wilderness must wrestle with the complicated issues surrounding the role of religion and spirituality in the public sphere.

NOTES

1. By wilderness *qua* wilderness I mean wilderness *as* wilderness, rather than wilderness as a store of natural resources, or wilderness as a venue for exercise and social bonding, or wilderness as a source of aesthetic experiences, and so on. The sense in which I use the term 'wilderness' will be clear after I uncomplicate it in chapter 1. Investigating the value of wilderness *qua* wilderness is investigating the value of the untrammeled natural world; of land retaining its primeval characteristics; of parts of the earth insignificantly influenced by human activity—past or present, intentional or unintentional, conspicuous or inconspicuous. Wilderness is a condition of the natural world, and the places called 'wilderness' comprise a domain marked by this condition. In posing the question of the value of wilderness *qua* wilderness, I am asking: what is the value of a domain marked by this condition?

2. A *pro tanto* reason is a reason that favors performing a certain action; it is not necessarily a decisive reason for that action, and it does not preclude the possibility of important reasons not to performing the action. Maria Alvarez gives a helpful illustration: "The fact that a joke is funny may be a reason to tell it; but the fact that it'll embarrass someone may be a reason against doing so. In that case, I have a *pro-tanto* reason to tell the joke and a different *pro-tanto* reason not to tell it" (Alvarez 2017).

Chapter One

Uncomplicating the Idea of Wilderness

Providing a generally satisfying definition of the wilderness has long been a contentious affair. Max Oelschlaeger put it best:

> Typically . . . those concerned with the idea of wilderness offer either a stipulative definition that suits their purposes or, more characteristically among scholars, a potpourri of positions. This second approach, though it sometimes achieves a near exhaustive listing, suffers from a lack of rigor and clarity. The idea of wilderness is whatever anyone or group cares to think. (Oelschlaeger 1991, 281)

Be that as it may, elaboration of some commonly accepted features of wilderness is a necessary first step toward a meaningful philosophical discussion of its ramifications. This task is complicated by the fact that a meta-debate has dominated the philosophical literature on the idea of wilderness for the past thirty years.[1] Though all parties to the debate express respect and admiration for those places that conventionally fall under the rubric 'wilderness,' a generation of scholars has found the idea of wilderness problematic, even objectionable, on several fronts. While some observers have found the debate to be stale, or misguided, or unimportant (e.g., Rolston 1998 and Orr 2008), problems concerning the idea of wilderness are now an imposing feature of the environmental ethics landscape such that any author wishing to discuss wilderness must first take a position on this debate.

Each time I've spoken publicly on the moral complexity of wilderness preservation, the first comment has inevitably been some variant of: "But there is no such thing as wilderness." I explain that by wilderness I simply mean something like the 'untrammeled land' of the 1964 Wilderness Act definition, parts of nature that are largely, if not entirely, free from human interference. If told this is too imprecise, I say I mean something like a condition of the natural world distinguished by a relative absence of human activity (past or present, intentional or unintentional, conspicuous or inconspicuous). I say that on the basis of ordinary language and much technical and legal language, 'wilderness' seems an appropriate, if not perfect, term to capture this concept and to enable conversation about what to do with and how to feel about the parts of world to which it is appropriately applied. But rather than returning to the subject of my talk, I am accused of promoting a specious human/nature divide, or told that such an idea of wilderness is culturally arrogant, or informed that the term has no referent, or asked why I think idle philosophical speculation is going to help wild places and wild animals. It appears the wilderness debate does indeed rage on.[2] A careful response to some persistent objections is needed.

My goal in this chapter is to uncomplicate the idea of wilderness such that it will be easier to discuss philosophical issues pertaining to areas of the natural world conventionally, and not unreasonably or arbitrarily, picked out the term 'wilderness' in subsequent chapters. Seeing our way past some of the misguided complications pertaining to the idea of wilderness will make it easier to attend to the legitimate complications—particularly the normative variety—that *do* merit continued scrutiny.

My method of uncomplication is to explain and respond to five objections to the idea of wilderness that, in addition to popping up in Q&A sessions, pervade the literature. These objections are (1) empirical, (2) cultural/ethnic/racial, (3) philosophical (4) social constructivist, (5) environmental/political. I argue that none of these objections constitutes a serious problem for the received idea of wilderness such that a philosopher wishing to explore the value of wild places and consider the import of moral problems accompanying their existence need be concerned that the project is sandbagged by a conceptual impasse.

To be clear: the idea of wilderness has difficulties, and I do not claim otherwise. What I do claim is that it is not nearly as complicated as some thinkers have made it out to be, and not for some of the reasons they give. The objections to the idea of wilderness discussed in this chapter should not forestall philosophical discussion of about the function and value of wilderness in environmental philosophy.

WILDERNESS AND NATURE

Much of the criticism of the idea of wilderness has been criticism of the idea as expressed in the U.S. Wilderness Act:

> A wilderness . . . is hereby recognized as an area where the earth and its community of life are untrammeled by man, where man himself is a visitor who does

not remain. [It is] land retaining its primeval character and influence, without permanent improvements or human habitation, which is protected and managed so as to preserve its natural conditions and which generally appears to have been affected primarily by the forces of nature, with the imprint of man's work substantially unnoticeable. (Wilderness Act 1964)

Indeed, it is the Wilderness Act definition that has been impugned as "the received wilderness concept."[3] Craig DeLancey takes it for granted that "it has been recognized that the concept of a wilderness as a region 'untrammeled' by human beings has a number of intractable difficulties," and as a consequence "there has been no consensus on how we should understand wilderness" (DeLancey 2012, 25). I agree that there is a lack of consensus, but lack of consensus does not imply intractable difficulties, especially when much of the difficulty is a function of misplaced criticism. Misplaced criticism does not become germane simply by being sustained for multiple decades.

To be sure, there may be legitimate concerns about the language of the Wilderness Act definition. Use of the term 'man,' for example, rather than 'humans' or 'humanity' is understandably objectionable to some contemporary readers. Another example: to the extent that to trammel something is to damage or misuse it, 'untrammeled' is an unavoidably evaluative term requiring a cultural, historical, and value-laden interpretation.[4] But whether the term should (or could) be optimized for the purposes of academic philosophy, there is a workable and useful idea adequately captured by the Wilderness Act definition as is stands, and it is this idea rather than the exact language of the Wilderness Act definition that often is, and may continue to be, suspected of intractable difficulties.

The objections I face when discussing wilderness are the same whether I use the language of the Wilderness Act or a semantically equivalent variant, and the objections always pertain to the idea of wilderness as the natural world distinguished by a relative absence of human activity (past or present, intentional or unintentional, conspicuous or inconspicuous). This is what is meant by the phrase "land retaining its primeval character." It is a factual statement, not a value judgement, that some areas of the earth have been shaped by humans forces (rather than natural) to a greater extent than others, regardless of whether one takes this to be good, bad, or neutral, and despite the fact that land often appearing as "primeval" to some observers turns out to have been walked on, worked, and altered by humans a great deal (more on this later). This idea of wilderness is plainly the essence of the Wilderness Act definition, and it is this idea—not a value-laden, potentially misanthropic, historically conditioned idea of "untrammeled" land as morally desirable or spiritually uplifting—with which many who work with the received wilderness idea, including myself, are actually interested.[5] I am responding to objections aimed at the facet of the Wilderness Act definition concerned with land "primarily shaped by the forces of nature." If successful, I will not have satisfied all concerns about the idea of wilderness or the Wilderness Act definition, but I will have uncomplicated the idea of wilderness in at least five ways. This uncomplication will make it easier to discuss a variety of philosophical topics associated with wilderness like, say, the fundamental value associated with preserving areas of the natural world largely shaped by natural rather than human forces, or the moral difficulties such areas present for human and animal populations.

Given that the idea of wilderness makes use of the idea of nature, let me briefly state how the latter term is used in this book. I follow a distinction between two senses of 'nature' drawn by J. S. Mill. In the first sense—call it 'Nature$_1$,'—'nature' is taken to mean:

> the aggregate of the powers and properties of all things. Nature means the sum of all phenomena, together with the causes which produce them; including not only all that happens, but all that is capable of happening; the unused capabilities of causes being as much a part of the idea of Nature, as those which take effect. (Mill 2000, 224)

The only way for an entity or a state of affairs to avoid being natural in this first sense is for it to be supernatural. When people point out that everything is natural, often to discredit the distinction between the natural and the unnatural utilized in environmental philosophy, they mean everything is part of Nature$_1$. In the second sense, Mill writes, "Nature is opposed to Art, and natural to artificial" (ibid.). Call this 'Nature$_2$.' Nature$_2$ does not contradict Nature$_1$, nor does it imply that art and the artificial are supernatural. All artifacts are natural in the first sense of the term. Iron worked by a blacksmith does not take on essentially different properties than iron left in the ground, though its natural properties and powers may have been manipulated or harnessed such that it now exhibits dispositions that the unworked metal does not have. As Mill writes, "Phenomena produced by human agency, no less, than those which as far as we are concerned are spontaneous, depend on the properties of the elementary forces, or of the elementary substances and their compounds." (ibid., 224–25). Going forward, I use the terms 'nature,' 'natural,' and 'natural world' to refer to the non-artificial, i.e., Nature$_2$.

THE EMPIRICAL OBJECTION

"The empirical objection to the wilderness idea," writes Keeling, "is straightforwardly simple: the wilderness idea is a non-issue for environmental ethics because there is no place left anywhere on the face of the earth that is completely free of human agency" (Keeling 2008, 506). If wilderness is to be understood as some kind of untrammeled land, or as the natural world absolutely unaffected by human activity, and if no such places exist, then there is no wilderness about which to debate. Without an actual referent, the term 'wilderness' is of no more consequence to environmental ethics than the island of Avalon or the lost continent of Atlantis. Bill McKibben advances the empirical objection in *The End of Nature* (McKibben 1990).[6] Humans have eradicated wilderness in conventional ways: fishing, farming, mining, settling and the like. But, McKibben argues, now that we have irreversibly interfered with the planetary climate, we can claim, without exaggeration, to have interfered with the entire earth to such an extent that wilderness is no longer possible.

Responses to the Empirical Objection

Dale Jamieson takes issue with McKibben's proclamation that nature, and wilderness, are no more. Even if "it is true that human interference with the climate system is affecting every part of the planet . . . it doesn't follow from this that we are at the 'end of nature'" (Jamieson 2008, 163). First, as Jamieson points out, such a claim is trivially false "since there is virtually no human influence on most of the universe" (ibid.). More important, however, is to recognize that the strength of empirical objections like McKibben's dissolves once we acknowledge that there is no reason why we cannot (and in fact do) understand nature and wilderness as existing by degree (cf. Birnbacher 2014).

It is possible for a place to be more or less of a wilderness depending upon the degree of past or present human influence that it has undergone. There are probably very few absolute wildernesses left on earth, but talk of wilderness does not become meaningless even if this is true. The Alaskan National Wildlife Refuge is wilderness to a greater degree than Walden Pond; Walden Pond is wilderness to a greater degree than the Boston Common; and the Boston Common is wilderness to a greater degree than Logan Airport even though none of these places is entirely free of human influence.

Lastly, Scott Friskics has convincingly argued that those who criticize the received wilderness idea, and who point to the 1964 US Wilderness act as the idea's paradigmatic example, are guilty of misreading. If one is troubled by an understanding of wilderness that enshrines an idea of a pristine never-touched-by-human-hands natural world, then one need not be troubled by its definition in the Wilderness Act. "This understanding of wilderness is not the one reflected in the Wilderness Act of 1964 or subsequent wilderness legislation" (Friskics 2008, 397–98). Not only is the idea of purity not built into the paradigmatic example of the received wilderness idea, but only "the most inattentive or unreflective wilderness visitors" would claim that absolute purity and a pristine natural condition are what they expect or experience when visiting the wilderness (ibid., 398).

The empirical objection should not concern us because, even in the absence of an absolute nature$_2$, we can meaningfully and usefully employ the term wilderness to refer to areas of the natural world characterized by a relative absence of human activity and influence, areas comprised of natural things and shaped by natural processes relative to those areas comprised of human artifacts and shaped by human activity. Furthermore, criticism of the received wilderness idea may be targeting a straw man given that neither wilderness legislation nor ordinary usage of the concept of wilderness relies on an absolute conception.

THE CULTURAL/ETHNIC/RACIAL OBJECTION

The cultural/ethnic/racial objection to the idea of wilderness (hereafter referred to simply as the cultural objection) claims that the received wilderness idea is a dangerous fiction emanating from Western ethnocentrism, racial insensitivity, and cultural myopia. It is potentially more damning than the empirical objection because, in addition to saying that wilderness does not exist, it says that the idea itself is pernicious inasmuch as it perpetuates the ethnocentrism and cultural insensitivity from which it arose.

Guha draws attention to the fact that it is American environmentalism, rather than simply environmentalism, that focuses on wilderness preservation (Guha 1998). His argument (to which I return in the discussion of the environmental/political objection) largely concerns the economic and political ramifications of trying to export American environmentalism to the so-called Third World (what today scholars today might refer to as the developing world or the Global South). At the same time, however, he highlights the extent to which a "preoccupation with wilderness preservation" is a Western, first world, and in the words of Roderick Nash, a "full stomach" phenomenon (ibid., 241, 238). Guha chafes at the suggestion of some Western biologists that they and only they should decide what happens to tropical ecosystems and who, if anyone, gets to live there (ibid., 235). To his ear, the idea of wilderness, and the drive for wilderness preservation, smacks of a new kind of imperialism. (A more charitable reaction on Guha's part would have understood the biologists to be saying that decisions about the future of tropical ecosystems should be made by experts, whatever their racial and national origins.)

Gomez-Pompa and Kaus advance a related claim in "Taming the Wilderness Myth." They write: "the concept of wilderness as an area without people has influenced thought and policy throughout the development of the western world" despite the fact that "recent research indicates that much wilderness has long been influenced by human activities" (Gomez-Pompa and Kaus 1998, 295). Moreover, "The concept of wilderness as the untouched or untamed land is mostly an urban perception, the view of people who are far removed from the natural environment they depend on for raw resources" (ibid., 297). In support of this claim, they cite an informal survey in which fifteen inhabitants of rural Mexico claim not to know what is meant by 'conservation,' despite, presumably, being good conservationists (ibid., 306). Gomez-Pompa and Kaus go further than Guha, however, in suggesting that Western biologists who advocate wilderness preservation are wrong to privilege science over traditional wisdom. "Scientific findings," they tell us, "are often accepted as if they are gospel word. But a scientific truth is really a conclusion drawn from a limited data set" (ibid., 295).

J. Baird Callicott adds to the cultural objection by claiming that the received wilderness idea rests on the mistaken belief that North America was a wilderness prior to 1492; as such, the idea becomes woefully ethnocentric by ignoring the influence of aboriginal people (Callicott 1998, 339, 348–49). Early European visitors to North America only conceived of the land as a wilderness because they were ignorant of what previous people had done to change the land, or, more nefariously, because they refused to recognize the earlier inhabitants as people having a culture.

Similar to Callicott, William Cronon laments the way nineteenth-century European Americans removed Indians "to create 'uninhabited wilderness'— uninhabited as never before in the human history of the place" (Cronon 1995, 480). And in line with Gomez-Pompa and Kaus, he contends: "The dream of an unworked natural landscape is very much the fantasy of people who have never themselves had to work the land to make a living" (ibid., 482). For Cronon, "there is nothing natural about the concept of wilderness" (ibid., 481).

Responses to the Culture Objection

Responding to the cultural objection is a delicate matter for two reasons. First, critiquing the cultural objection opens the critic up to charges of ethnocentrism and cultural arrogance. But more important, it is possible (and I think necessary) to accept the charge that a cultural bias often motivates concern for the wilderness while rejecting the relevance of that motivation to philosophical questions concerning the essence and value of wilderness.

Guha is right to point out that American environmentalism places a higher value on wilderness preservation than, say, environmentalism in his native India. As he explains, environmentalism in the developing world has a greater focus on cleaning up rivers, slowing deforestation, and improving air quality. Likewise, Gomez-Poma and Kaus are correct to suggest that Western biologists should consult with, and seek to learn from, indigenous populations in the places they wish to study and save. But these reasonable points do not discredit the idea of wilderness as the natural world characterized by a relative absence of human activity and influence.

If the cultural objection means to suggest that the received wilderness idea is flawed simply because it was developed in the West, by Europeans and white Americans, then it commits the genetic fallacy; the veracity and value of an idea cannot be assessed solely on the idea's point of origin. Moreover, even if the idea of wilderness and wilderness preservation is foreign to some indigenous people, as Gomez-Pompa and Kaus maintain, it is unclear how that makes the idea philosophically problematic. Presumably the fifteen inhabitants of rural Mexico cited by Gomez-Pompa and Kaus were also ignorant of *modus tollens* and the law of the excluded middle, yet this neither makes the rural Mexicans illogical nor the elementary rules of logic unreal and ethnocentric. At *most* we could say the idea of wilderness was first conceived and employed and by people of European decent (though that is far from certain), in which case it is not much different from the idea of calculus or radio waves.

Callicott and Cronon are in the same boat as Guha, Gomez-Pompa, and Kaus: their cultural critique of the wilderness idea is apt without being philosophically damaging. It is true that North America was not an uninhabited, absolute wilderness in 1492, and it is true that Europeans and Americans have often applied the term 'wilderness' in ways that are culturally arrogant and racially insentive. Notice, though, that the tendency to miss or discount the influence of certain groups of humans does not in any way indicate that there is something wrong with the idea of wilderness as the natural world largely uninfluenced by human activity. It just means one ought to be very careful before labeling someone else's land a wilderness for the purpose of furthering one's own aims (whatever these aims might be), and that one should look more carefully at the way other people, in other cultures, have lived with and transformed nature.

No one can reasonably deny that racism and cultural arrogance pervaded much European exploration and colonization in North America. Yet, as Rolston argues, this fact alone does not mean that the ascription of wilderness conditions to the new world by Europeans is an unjustified act of racism. In the fifteenth century, the North American continent was wilderness to a greater degree than Britain, France, Spain, Portugal, and The Netherlands given the limited cultural capacity of indigenous Americans to remake nature *relative* to the capacity of Europeans at the same time. To point this out slanders neither the character or racial quality of indigenous Americans, nor "disparages aboriginal Indian culture" (Rolston 1998, 377–79). We know that some European settlers, despite their advanced technology and supposedly superior cultures, would have not made it past their first few years in the New World without the practical wisdom and generosity of some indigenous groups.

We can grant that, historically, some have taken factual claims about American Indian culture as grounds for making evaluative judgments about the people themselves—both positive and negative. What I am pointing out is that one can and really should separate the factual from the evaluative. To say that fifteenth-century Europeans had a greater power to remake nature than the inhabitants of what became fifteenth-century New England does not logically entail a positive evaluation of one group and negative evaluation of the other. A further argument would be needed, and I, for one, see no reason to give it.

One other feature of the cultural objection deserves comment, namely, the anti-scientific stance it sometimes adopts. Gomez-Pompa and Kaus write: "Scientific findings are often accepted as if they are gospel word. But a scientific truth is really a conclusion drawn from a limited data set" (Gomez-Pompa and Kaus 1998, 295). It is a common tactic among those who favor the cultural critique to go beyond the reasonable claim that many Western environmentalists have been guilty of cultural arrogance and implicit bias when dealing with non-Western people in non-Western regions, and to then begin attacking science and reason *qua* science and reason as yet another example of ethnocentric imperialism. This is a worrying tactic that ought to be resisted.

To claim that scientific findings are accepted as if they are gospel is to badly misunderstand both science and the Gospels. In fact, one could not choose a worse analogy. The Gospels are accepted as if they are gospel—no additional evidence, no verification, and no falsification is needed or sought. Scientific knowledge, to the contrary, warrants all three. And so long as scientists are operating in good faith, they will be the first to admit that their conclusions are never absolute and only one experiment or one field survey away from revision.

It is not inaccurate to say that a scientific truth is a conclusion drawn from a limited data set. But how is that a criticism? This *modus operandi* is what makes a scientific conclusion so pointedly different from a conclusion accepted as if it were gospel truth (the Gospels being, for some Christian believers, a complete data set that requires no revision and admits no falsification). Western environmentalism and conservation biology deserve to have their cultural and racial biases exposed as much as any other human endeavor. But let us not throw the baby out with the bathwater and begin dismissing science as naught but Western arrogance, or like Gary Snyder, put the term 'enlightenment' in scare quotes to indicate that we ought not take the European emphasis on reason too seriously (Snyder 2008, 552). Nor, to revive a point made by John Passmore more than four decades ago, should we suppose that a turn to mysticism or spirituality—Western or Eastern—will provide a panacea for looming environmental crises. Environmentally deleterious applications of reason and science do not constitute an argument for the abandonment of these traditions. To the contrary, global environmental problems call for more reason and better science (Passmore 1974). There is also something unintentionally demeaning in coupling a rejection of reason and science with an admiration for (and dubious appropriation of) non-Western or indigenous traditions.[7]

THE PHILOSOPHICAL OBJECTION

The idea of wilderness depends upon a distinction between humans or the human world and nature or the natural world. The philosophical objection to the idea of wilderness is, as Keeling expresses it, "that its idealization of pristine, untrammeled nature enshrines an untenable human/nature dualism. To say that a wilderness area protects the 'forces of nature' by excluding 'human works,' is to presuppose that nature and human artifacts belong to mutually exclusive ontological categories" (Keeling 2008, 506). If the wilderness idea does depend on human/nature dualism, and if this dualism is philosophically untenable, then the idea of wilderness is untenable.

For Cronon, the philosophical objection is the "central paradox" of the whole issue because the received idea of "wilderness embodies a dualistic vision in which the human is entirely outside the natural" (Cronon 1995, 482). Moreover, "The dualism at the heart of wilderness encourages its advocates to conceive of its protection as a crude conflict between the 'human' and the 'nonhuman'" (ibid., 486). For Callicott, the wilderness idea relies on a pre-Darwinian Western metaphysical dichotomy of man and nature (Callicott 1998, 348). But since we know that "man is a natural, a wild, an evolving species, not essentially different in this respect from all the others . . . then the works of man, however precocious are as natural as those of beavers, or termites" (ibid., 350). From this Callicott concludes that human interference in the natural world cannot be anything other than natural, and the concept of wilderness, relying as it does on a distinction between the human and the natural, cannot be maintained.

Steven Vogel is perhaps the staunchest advocate of the philosophical objection. For him, "the sharp distinction between nature and artifact doesn't hold up," rendering the idea of wilderness as the natural world minus the influence of man a mere "stipulative definition" (Vogel 2003, 152). He calls our attention to the human acts of "digging, planting, weeding, and burning." "When looked at carefully," he writes, "all the processes these actions put into place themselves are wild" (ibid., 162). For Vogel this phenomenon raises an unanswerable question: "why are those processes called natural ones, while the ones we initiate are not?" (ibid., 152). Finally, Vogel advises that "if we begin to think even more carefully, we might come to see that the wild is always there in all our acts, and in all our artifacts" (ibid., 163).

Responses to the Philosophical Objection

As with previous objections, the philosophical objection takes a partial truth and draws a specious conclusion. Contrary to Callicott, the wilderness idea does not rely on a peculiar metaphysical dualism, nor does it stand in opposition to a Darwinian account of the evolutionary origin of *Homo sapiens*. And contrary to Vogel, we can explain why certain processes are called 'natural' or 'wild' while others are not. Furthermore, the fact that the distinctions between wild and non-wild, nature and artifice, are not always sharp is not an insurmountable difficulty; rather, it means wilderness has vagueness not unlike many other terms meaningfully explored and employed by philosophy.

Rolston is adamant that the philosophical objection presents "no cause for being negative about wilderness," given that "One hardly needs metaphysics or theology to realize that there are critical differences between wild nature and human culture" (Rolston 1998, 367, 268). Animals, on the one hand, "are what they are genetically, instinctively, environmentally, without any options at all." Humans, on the other hand, "have a myriad of lifestyle options, evidenced by their cultures; and each human makes daily decisions that affect his or her character. Little or nothing in nature approaches this" (ibid., 368). Animals may have "freedom within ecosystems," but humanity is uniquely distinguished by having "freedom from ecosystems." No longer part of biological evolution by means of natural selection, humanity adapts ecosystems to meet its needs; animals, however, must adapt to their ecological niche (ibid., 368). Rolston elaborates:

> Animals do not hold elections and plan their environmental affairs; they do not make bulldozers to cut down tropical rainforests. They do not fund development projects through the World Bank or contribute to funds to save the whales. They do not teach their religion to their children. They do not write articles revisiting and reaffirming the idea of wilderness. They do not get confused about whether their actions are natural or argue about whether they can improve nature. (Ibid., 369)

None of this requires a metaphysical or theological belief in an immaterial soul or the intrinsic separateness and superiority of humankind from the rest of creation. If these differences, and the countless left unnamed, are not justification for drawing a distinction between humanity and wild nature, then it is hard to know what could count, short of strict logical necessity, as a justification for drawing distinctions of any kind between any things.

If by saying that we are not "essentially" different from other creatures, Callicott simply means that humans too are carbon-based life-forms, subject to the laws of physics, comprised of the same elemental materials as the rest of the universe, then he is correct. We are all part of nature$_1$, as Mill pointed out. But this is a fact that no one would deny, least of all proponents of the wilderness idea. Rolston is right: "If there is metaphysical confusion in this debate" it lies in the belief that affirming the aforementioned scientific truths creates a metaphysical problem for those wishing to draw a distinction between the wild and the not wild given that the distinction between nature$_1$ and nature$_2$ is tenable (ibid., 369).

Keeling employs a different strategy to rebuff the philosophical objection. Appealing to Wittgenstein's notion of language games, he argues that the terms 'wild' and 'wilderness' perform a particular, perfectly understandable function. The terms only become problematic if we seek to break or change the rules of the game we are playing. According to Keeling, the wilderness idea is committed to the following proposition:

P1—No human artifacts are natural$_2$.

Callicott and Vogel worry that P1 contradicts ecological holism—the view that humankind and human works are evolutionary phenomena no less natural than the works of beavers and termites. If ecological holism is correct, then Callicott and Vogel feel they must endorse a different proposition:

P2—All human artifacts are natural$_2$.

Thus the philosophical objection appears to leave us with a contradiction, Cronon's "central paradox." Keeling sees the objection as a red herring, one that "relies on unexamined assumptions about language, and on specific assumptions about what the word 'nature' means" (Keeling 2008, 508). Ecological holism needn't dissolve into ecological monism.

Rather than trying to intuit the essential meaning of 'wilderness' and 'nature,' Keeling believes we should seek out the function of the terms. "It would be more profitable," he writes, "to approach this intractable problem by treating language not just as a way of referring to things . . . but also as . . . a kind of rule-guided practice" (ibid., 508). Like Wittgenstein, he wants us to accept that "highly ramified abstract nouns (like 'nature') should be thought of in terms of their purpose rather than their 'meaning'" (ibid., 508). The question "Is *x* wild?" or "Is *x* natural?" lacks the context needed for us to have much idea what is being asked or how to answer.

Keeling encourages us to put the question in context, and then provides several examples to illustrate his point. Consider the following utterances (all quoted from ibid., 510):

- "We are using a natural process to trigger these avalanches" (announcing a proposal to trigger avalanches with explosive)
- "This is a natural lake" (pointing to a lake formed by a hydroelectric dam)
- "What a stunning place, isn't nature beautiful" (from within the inside of a cathedral)
- "It's amazing what nature can do" (pointing to a computer)

The proper response to these utterances would be confusion, something like: *"What are you talking about?"* One who hears them would assume that either the speaker is making mistakes, or that they lack an elementary understanding of the language. The utterances are meaningful, but only if you accept some sort of natural/not natural distinction. As it happens, this distinction is already present and habitually employed in the language game we are playing.

Vogel's question "Why are these processes called natural ones, while ones we initiate are not?" (imagine Vogel referring to plate tectonics and beavers building dams) is, as Keeling puts it, akin to asking: "Why do we say that black is darker than white?" There is no answer we can give beyond trying to explain that this is simply how the words are used. "There is no way to justify empirically the fact that human artifacts are not natural objects" (ibid., 511).

Keeling aptly notes that Vogel's attempt to deny or radically change the meaning of wilderness "is (not unlike poetry) simply to invent a new context for the word 'wild' where there are no established rules for its use" (ibid., 512). Rolston makes a similar complaint about Callicott: "Poets like Gary Snyder perhaps are entitled to poetic license. But philosophers are not, especially when analyzing the concept of wildness" (Rolston 1998, 369). If one does not like using the term 'wilderness' to designate specific parts of the natural world characterized by their lack of human activity and influence, one is free to suggest another term. Terms change all the time for various political, cultural, and scientific reasons. 'African-American' replaced 'black,' which replaced 'colored,' and so on. But whether we use the term 'wilderness' or some other combination of shapes and sounds, we can still meaningfully speak of and think about the natural world free, or relatively free, from human activity and influence. What we cannot reasonably do is begin playing a new, spontaneous language game such that a term generates paradox and then fault others for falling prey to this new paradox.

There is clearly a sense in which human beings are just another part of nature (we are biological organisms descended from the same tree of life as every other creature), yet this lineage does not mean that it is unreasonable to talk about a human/nature divide. Indeed, the entire project of environmental ethics depends upon our ability to conceptually distinguish ourselves from nature$_2$ so that we can reflect upon the norms that ought to guide our relations with the nonhuman world. By some accounts, sex and gender are also vague concepts that get fuzzy at the edges, but this property does not mean we should not engage with feminist ethics or queer theory simply because, in some sense, all human beings are the same. If one truly believes that there is no meaningful distinction between humans and the rest of nature, then the project of environmental ethics should be abandoned. Serious ethical problems might also arise within societies as it would be hard to ground concepts like responsibility or legal liability.

THE SOCIAL CONSTRUCTIVIST OBJECTION

The social constructivist objection rests on the belief that wilderness is not real because nature is not real; nature has no independent reality and is merely a socially constructed phenomenon. In this way it is similar to the cultural objection. But whereas the cultural objection need not take the extreme view that nature itself is a cultural product, this is precisely what the social constructivist critique maintains: nature and wilderness are artifacts. If wilderness is an artifact, then the idea of wilderness as the natural world retaining its primeval characteristics, insignificantly influenced by human activity, makes no sense. The social constructivist objection is a curious reversal of the empirical objection. Whereas the empirical objection states that wilderness once existed but no longer does due to the activities of humankind, the social constructivist objection states that wilderness never existed until humankind created it. There is a weaker version of the social constructivist objection that states that only the *ideas* of nature and wilderness are constructed, not the objects from which the idea arise. This distinction is rarely maintained in the literature.

Cronon encapsulates the social constructivist position when he writes: "Far from being the one place on earth that stands apart from humanity, it [wilderness] is quite profoundly a human creation" (Cronon 1995, 471). Then, like every other critic of the wilderness idea, he hastens to express his commitment to wild places: "By now I hope it is clear that my criticism . . . is not directed at wild nature per se, or even at efforts to set aside large tracts of wild land, but rather at the specific habits of thinking that flow from this *cultural construction called 'wilderness'*" (ibid., 483 emphasis mine).

In *The Social Creation of Nature*, Neil Evernden claims "We are going to have to admit our own role in the constitution of reality" such that we "might even say that there is no 'nature,' and there never has been" (Evernden 1992, 60, 24). Along the same lines, he adds: "Before the word [nature] was invented, there was no nature" (ibid., 89). The wilderness, therefore, is "As much an artifact as a traffic light" (ibid., 94). He sums up his position grandiloquently: "History and culture do not rest on nature, nature rests on history and culture" (ibid., 99).

John O'Neill, although not himself a strong social constructivist, provides further examples of the social constructivist view in "Wilderness, Cultivation, and Appropriation" (O'Neill 2002). He cites Catherine Larrere's claim that "Nature per se does not exist. . . . Nature is only the name given to a certain contemporary state of science," and Don Cupitt's observation that "We have no basis for distinguishing between Nature and our own changing historically-produced representation of nature—Nature is a cultural product" (ibid., 528). O'Neill then suggests that the ideas of Larrere and Cupitt find their intellectual footing in Derrida's contention: "There is nothing outside the text." If O'Neill is correct, this would explain the antipathy of so many environmental writers toward postmodernism, and the reason postmodernism is often targeted by proponents of the environmental/political objection.

Response to the Social Constructivist Objection

The primary mistake made by the social constructivist objection is to takes an uncontroversial point concerning the social construction of knowledge and push it too far. As Eileen Crist has observed, "the idea that knowledge is socio-historically situated seems trivially true," but "probing into the assumption and repercussions of the 'social construction of nature' reveals it to be intellectually narrow" (Crist 2004, 6). To point out that an idea has a particular social, cultural, and historical genesis, and to further point out that we humans can only access the idea socially, culturally, and historically, does not entail that the entity or state of affairs picked out by the idea lacks independent reality. To maintain otherwise would be to say that iron didn't exist until humanity possessed the idea of iron, or that a species does not exist until it is discovered and socially constructed. I do not intend to give a robust defense of this last assertion as it would change this from a work on environmental philosophy to a work on metaphysics and epistemology, yet surely the burden of proof lies with the proponent of a strong social constructivist idealism.

One can acknowledge that ideas are, in some sense, the product of social construction without needing to conclude that nothing beyond our socially constructed ideas exists. The mediated, socially constrained aspect of human knowledge of the natural world does not lead to the conclusion that before the word 'nature' was invented, that to which nature refers did not exist. As O'Neill neatly puts the matter:

> For the strong constructivist, once we are made aware of the cultural origins of our responses we realize that there is no 'nature' there, that we are surrounded by a world of cultural objects. That strong constructivism is mistaken. . . . There is a clear distinction to be drawn between the sources of our attitudes, which are economic, political and cultural, and the objects of our attitudes which can still remain non-cultural. (O'Neill 2008, 539)

David Orr calls our attention to the fact that if the social constructivists are right, they have some explaining to do. "Most surely," he writes, "we see Nature through the lens of culture, class, and circumstances. Even so it is remarkable how similarly Nature is in fact 'constructed' across different classes, cultures, times, and circumstances" (Orr 2008, 431). If nature is in fact socially constructed, we should at least account for the uncanny similarity of its construction across time and space. For Orr the answer is obvious: "gravity, sunlight, geology, soil, animals, and the biogeochemical cycles of the earth" have independent realities that dictate the way we construct them (ibid., 431).

To take seriously the belief that wilderness and nature are socially constructed would require an error theory. This error theory would have to explain the universal experiential difference between observing and interacting with a bear in a zoo and a bear in the wild. Daniel Dombrowski argues that if the social constructivists are right, then there is no significant difference between a zoo and the wilderness, and thus there ought be no significant difference between our experiences of a bear in the wild and a bear in the zoo. But there is a world of phenomenological difference between these two experiences. Both may inspire feelings of curiosity and excitement, but only one gives rise to experience of fear, mortal danger, and even the sublime (Dombrowski 2002, 200). Such a differences should not exist if wilderness cannot be distinguished from a zoo, if the artifice cannot be distinguished from the natural. Until an adequate error theory is forthcoming from the social constructivists, we should not hesitate to maintain the reality of wilderness.

The social constructivist objection can safely be dismissed in its strong form—the objects of nature are socially constructed—and its weak form—our ideas of the objects of nature are socially constructed. Only the latter has plausibility, yet as Rolston puts it: "There is always some sort of cognitive framework within which nature makes its appearance, but that does not mean that what appears is only the framework" (quoted in Dombrowski 2002, 199). And it is a strange logical leap to go from the premise 'All ideas are socially constructed' to the conclusion 'Socially constructed ideas should not be taken seriously' or 'Socially constructed ideas are not based on an objective referent.'

THE ENVIRONMENTAL OBJECTION

The final objection I want to consider is the environmental objection. The environmental objection is distinguished from the four preceding objections in that it does not necessarily claim that there is something erroneous about the idea of wilderness. Instead, this objection opposes any further debate on the idea of wilderness on the grounds that the debate does not contribute to the achievement environmental goals and might in fact inhibit the political action to which the true environmentalist should be attending. On this view, the only role for environmental philosophy is to further the goals of environmental activism by cogently attacking the environmentalists' foes and offering *apologia* for environmentalists' agendas. Rather than debate the nature, meaning, and value of wilderness, we should get out there and save what wilderness is left. This, I take it, is what some audience members have meant when they claim that my attention to the moral complexity of wilderness preservation isn't helping wilderness.

Gary Snyder begins his essay "Is Nature Real?" with the following grievance: "I'm getting grumpy about the slippery arguments being put forth by high-paid intellectuals trying to knock nature and knock the people who value nature and still come out smelling smart and progressive" (Snyder 2008, 351). Later he suggests that academic work in the humanities and social sciences on, *inter alia*, the extent to which nature is a part of culture and culture just a part of nature, might be "just a strategy to keep the budget within their specialties . . ." (Ibid., 353). Orr, a critic of the wilderness debate, writes: "The question is whether environmentalists can offer practical, workable, and sensible ideas—not abstractions, arcane ideology, spurious dissent, and ideological hair-splitting reminiscent of 19th century socialists" (Orr 2008, 430). He asks us to put aside ideas that will "not be particularly useful for helping us create a sustainable and sustaining civilization," however useful such an idea "may be as a reason to organize conferences in exotic places and for keeping postmodernists employed at high-paying indoor jobs." We have no more need for "ivory tower" environmentalism (ibid., 431).

Callicott contributes to the environmental objection by arguing that the received wilderness idea prioritizes wilderness as the environmental ideal when some version of sustainable development or "land health" would be both easier to enact and better for the environment. "And if the concept of land health replaces the popular, conventional idea of wilderness as the standard of conservation, then we might begin to envision ways of creatively reintegrating man and nature" (Callicott 1998, 355).

Guha's main argument is that the wilderness idea is either inexpedient or inapplicable when exported to the so-called Third World. Thus, in addition to criticizing the wilderness idea for being culturally insensitive and racially imperialistic, Guha is criticizing it for failing to help us meet the environmental goals that most need to be met (Guha 1998).

Responses to the Environmental Objection

As with the cultural objection, the environmental objection makes some undeniably accurate claims that nonetheless remain irrelevant to the challenge of developing a philosophical conception of wilderness. For the sake of argument let us concede that academic debates on the meaning and value of wilderness have failed to advance the practical, political conservation goals of environmentalism. But so what? Such a criticism could only be a mark against the wilderness idea if the sole function of discussing such an idea was to advance a particular environmental agenda. Environmental philosophy should not necessarily be the servant of environmental activism, and to the extent that we have scholars asking hard questions rather than merely pushing political ends, the field is arguably moving in the right direction. Even if these hard questions foster a debate that fails to immediately save an endangered species or protect an old growth forest, I fail to see the problem for a *philosophical* investigation of the idea of wilderness.[8] Perhaps the objection is really a critique of philosophy and the supposedly "high-paid" intellectuals it employs.

While irrelevant to my argument, the claim that philosophical speculation about nature does not advance the environmentalist's cause is, it bears adding, false. It is straightforward intellectual history to trace the philosophical ruminations about the meaning and value of nature in, say, Emerson and Thoreau, to the political environmentalism of Muir, Pinchot, and Leopold. Nevertheless, my point remains: *qua* philosopher, Emerson's reflections on the meaning and value of nature are not properly judged by the extent to which Muir put them to use in the service of establishing Yosemite National Park.

Not only must environmentalists accept the fact that philosophy is not—and should not be—activism by other means, but they must also be open to the possibility that philosophical analysis of the natural world may result in conclusions that actually *are* inimical to the goals of mainstream environmentalism. Crucially, this fact alone should never be used to assess the quality or importance of the philosophy in question. Take the case of Jeff McMahan's "The Moral Problem of Predation" in which he argues, *inter alia*, for the potential desirability of germline genetic modification to transform carnivores to herbivores so that, one day, the lion may truly lie down with the lamb (McMahan 2015). Whatever one thinks of McMahan's conclusion, the article itself is a superb piece of philosophical reasoning. It makes an admirable contribution to our thinking about animal rights and environmental philosophy, and the contribution is not lessened by the fact that, if McMahan's argument is sound, it will entail undesirable consequences for much mainstream environmentalism.

Finally, Orr's accusation that the wilderness debate is too much like nineteenth-century socialism is itself troubling. Implicit in this characterization is the idea that a worthy movement is being hamstrung by academic discourse and in-fighting, and that what we really need is to throw off the thoughtfulness of Marx and Engels and find ourselves an environmental Lenin or Trotsky (though presumably not Stalin) to take charge, keep the intellectuals in line, and get things done. To repeat: such action *may* be desirable from the standpoint of environmental activism, but it is likely to slow and impede the progress of environmental philosophy.

CONCLUSION

I have tried to uncomplicate the idea of wilderness by responding to five objections that are, in many ways, misguided, irrelevant, and inaccurate. I do not claim, however, that the idea of wilderness is without legitimate complications. It may be worth considering whether the term wilderness is now so burdened with unwanted historical, political, and moral associations that we'd be better off without it. In other words, even though 'wilderness' does not present intractable difficulties such that philosopher cannot usefully employ the term, perhaps there are sufficient reasons why we should choose some other collection of shapes and sounds to refer to parts of the natural world marked by a relative absence of human activity and influence.[9] While I do not favor abandoning the term, such a conversation is worth having. What is vital is that it becomes easier to engage with philosophical problems associated with evaluating, preserving, augmenting, managing, or eliminating areas of the natural world that remain, relative to other parts of the natural world, largely shaped by natural rather than human forces. In 1984, Mark Sagoff was able to meaningfully discuss the moral plight of animals living in the wilderness and the extent to which environmental ethics and animal liberation are necessary at odds (Sagoff 1984). Should his article have come out today, a perceptive and provocative argument may well be obscured by empirical, cultural, social constructivist, philosophical, and environmental objections to his use of the term 'wilderness.' The idea of wilderness is sure to become complicated for new, unexpected reasons. But before the new complications arrive, we should let go of the five addressed here.

NOTES

1. The current debate can at least be traced to Ramachandra Guha's 1989 essay "Radical American Environmentalism and Wilderness Preservation: A Third World Critique" (Guha 1998).

2. Everyone interested in the philosophy of wilderness should read *Rethinking Wilderness*, by Mark Woods (Woods 2017). Woods's book is superb—insightful, lucid, and provocative—but I do not discuss it in this work. The research for *Wilderness, Morality, and Value* was done between 2014 and 2016, and the manuscript was written between 2016 and April 2018. I was unaware of Woods's book until long after I had finished writing my own. Our analyses and arguments have a degree of convergence on some issues; they also have substantial differences in scope, scale, and focus. Adequately engaging with Woods's robust study would require a writing a very different book from that which I feel needed to be written. Rather than give an insufficient, *post hoc* treatment of *Rethinking Wilderness*, I prefer to let *Wilderness, Morality, and Value* stand as it was conceived and composed. Better for the field, I think, to have two complementary, though distinct and independent, philosophical studies of wilderness than to have one book plus a commentary.

3. It was Callicott who first spoke of a "received wilderness concept" in reference to, and to criticize, the understanding of wilderness found in the 1964 US Wilderness Act. See Callicott 1998, 339, 349.

4. This general point about the potential evaluative dimension of conceptions of wilderness is brought out nicely in Kirchhoff and Vicenzotti's historical survey of European conceptions of wilderness (Kirchhoff and Vicenzotti 2014).

5. John Nagle's study of the legislative debate leading up to the passage of the Wilderness Act supports this interpretation. A primary reason given in support of the Wilderness Act was to preserve land as it was created by God. While there is an explicit theistic dimension to this reason that may raise another kind of concern about the Wilderness Act definition, 'land as created by God' was meant to capture the idea of land retaining its primeval character, that is, land as it was or could be prior to and free from human interference (Nagle 2005: 979). In "The Value of Nature's Otherness," Simon Hailwood reminds us that it is nature's otherness—its other-than-human quality—that is a source of interest and value. Distinction from rather than continuity with nature best explains some of our valuable encounters with the natural world (Hailwood 2000).

6. McKibben uses the term nature rather than wilderness, though what he means by nature is equivalent to what I mean by wilderness. Thus we can, without confusion, understand him as speaking of the end of wilderness.

7. Guha understandably bemoans the alacrity with which Western environmentalists have appropriated disparate Eastern religions to justify radical environmental goals, supposing that Eastern traditions can succeed where Western rationalism has failed. Implicit in this move is the suggestion that these non-Western traditions are valuable *because* they are less rational. Guha contends that the Western environmentalist's typical "reading of Eastern traditions is selective and does not bother to differentiate between alternate (and changing) religious and cultural traditions; as it stands it does considerable violence to the historical record" (Guha 1998, 237).

8. In *Letter on Humanism*, Heidegger makes a similar point on Marx's last thesis on Feuerbach. Even if it is true, as Marx claims, that the point of philosophy is not to understand the world but to change it, everything hangs on what one takes to be 'the world' (Heidegger 1949).

9. My thanks to Derek Turner for raising this point in conversation.

Chapter Two

The Moral Ambiguity of Wilderness Preservation

Chapter 1 established an understanding of wilderness and defended it against five persistent criticisms. Chapter 2 will argue that wilderness and the intentional preservation of wilderness is morally ambiguous. The moral ambiguity I am interested in is this: to protect and actively preserve wilderness is to protect and actively preserve a system that entails incalculable, unremitent suffering and early death for many millions of sentient beings; given that it is now in our power to alleviate some of this suffering, and given the likelihood that our ability to lessen this suffering will continue to improve, we should ask ourselves if it might now, or at some future point, be morally praiseworthy to oppose wilderness and morally blameworthy to protect it. At the very least, I aim to show that a moral argument in defense of wilderness is warranted, and that such an argument will require a reevaluation of the value of wilderness.

Not everyone will agree that a moral argument in defense of wilderness is warranted. Certainly few will agree that one is warranted in the way that, for example, most agree that a moral argument in defense of war is warranted. War is an acknowledged moral labyrinth, an enterprise now considered intrinsically morally repugnant but occasionally morally permissible and even more occasionally morally required. Wilderness and the preservation of wilderness, however, have no such acknowledged association. If anything, it is opposition to wilderness that is generally thought to require a moral defense, and opposition to wilderness preservation that must make a moral case. I will argue that we have a *pro tanto* reason to question the morality of wilderness preservation, and that any defense of wilderness must first acknowledge the moral complexity of wilderness preservation and then offer an *apologia* based on the distinct value of wilderness *qua* wilderness.

Given that I am arguing that wilderness preservation can be and often is inimical to animal welfare, it is important to highlight that the contrary is usually taken to be the case; it is usually believed that wilderness preservation promotes animal welfare. This belief, represented by what I call the Argument from Welfare (AFW), is a prevalent and politically powerful defense that is regularly mustered to support wilderness preservation. I will first say something about the ubiquity of appeals to animal welfare among environmentalists and conservationists. I will then formalize and present the AFW, after which I will show how the AFW may be getting things the wrong way round by presenting what I call the Objection from Welfare (OFW). I will then consider four responses to the OFW.

I am not suggesting that wilderness preservation succeeds or fails solely on the merits of the AFW and OFW. Indeed, it will be the function the remaining chapters to reconsider other arguments for wilderness preservation, and, deeper than that, to question the fundamental value of wilderness *qua* wilderness with an eye toward understanding what kind of moral arguments on behalf of wilderness are possible. The narrow task for the present chapter is to show that we have at least one *pro tanto* reason to question the morality of wilderness and thus good cause to reconsider the value of wilderness and the strength of arguments made on its behalf.

ARGUMENTS FROM WELFARE IN ENVIRONMENTALISM

The Argument from Welfare, which will be explained at length in the following section, can be briefly stated as follows. Because we have a moral reason to concern ourselves with the welfare of animals, and because the destruction of wilderness is inimical to their welfare, we have a moral reason to preserve the wilderness. But given the variety of distinct arguments used to defend wilderness—Michael Nelson identifies thirty—why focus on the AFW (Nelson 1998)?

The first reason is that the AFW has become common moral currency among ideologically disparate environmentalists. Since the late nineteenth century—the time of John Muir and Gifford Pinchot—environmentalists have been unofficially grouped as preservationists and conservationists.[1] Both groups respect and care for the natural world. The difference between them concerns what one thinks about the value of nature and what one believes good environmental policy should hope to achieve. Speaking broadly, environmental conservationists (following Pinchot) believe that we should study and give stewardship to the natural world for the purpose of wise resource management. Environmental preservationists (following Muir) have tended to ascribe intrinsic value to the nonhuman natural world and believe that good environmental policy will seek to preserve nature as it is. Yet even when they agree on little else, heirs of Muir and Pinchot appear to agree that animal welfare is paramount.

The second reason to start with the AFW—and the reason that it has become ubiquitous among environmentalists—is its nonanthropocentric grounding. To say that the AFW is nonanthropocentric is to say it does not locate the value of wilderness solely in its value to human beings. As such, it is thought to be, in the words of conservation biologists Michael Soule and E. O. Wilson, less "ethically dubious" than anthropocentric arguments which determine the value of nature by reference to the value extracted by humans (Max 2014). The fact that the AFW has broad appeal while also seeming to rest on firm moral ground makes it an especially useful argument in the fight for wilderness. A series of articles from *Mongabay*, a prominent source for environmental journalism, illustrates the claim.

In the spring of 2016 *Mongabay* reported on a rift in the environmentalist community that has been growing for the past thirty years (Hance 2016). At issue was the value of nature and the best strategy with which to protect it. On one hand, those now called traditional conservationists (the historical analogue of preservationists) argue that nature is intrinsically valuable, and that best way to protect it is to acquire as much land as possible and then protect that land from human development and economic exploitation. On the other hand, those now called *new* conservationists (the historical analogue of conservationists), argue that nature is instrumentally valuable and that the best way to protect nature is to promote the sustainable exploitation of ecosystem resources and to work with rather than against big business. By 2014 the dispute had become so divisive that 238 biologists, ecologists, and environmentalists signed a petition pleading for détente.

The salient aspect of the debate for our purposes is that both sides claim that their primary focus is and always will be wildlife—as if to say that anything else would indicate a derangement of values and essentially cede the moral ground to their opponent.[2] Again and again the traditionalists charge that the new conservation has forgotten about wildlife. As environmental journalist Jeremy Hance puts it:

> They [traditionalists] contend that new conservationists have traded in programs focusing directly on wildlife for ones that may or may not help endangered species. And that by dropping arguments about morality and values, new conservationists have essentially handed the argument to nature utilitarians: if the rabbit has no economic value, kill the rabbit. In today's red in tooth and claw capitalism, nature must pay for itself. (Hance 2016, part 1 section 3)

And later:

"It's not tension. It's bewilderment," said Paul Salaman, the CEO of Rainforest Trust, when I [Hance] asked him about the tension between traditionalists and new conservationists. "Seriously, I understand that they want to look at different strategies," he said, but new conservation is "not really targeting the wildlife that needs help." (Hance 2016, part 1 section 10)

But the new conservationists repeatedly respond that this isn't so. "Deon Nel, the Global Conservation Director with WWF [an organization aligned with new conservation] insists the primary focus of the group 'will always be' wildlife," while Tom Dillon, also of WWF, maintains that new conservation is the "only way we will be able to protect the world's wildlife" (Hance 2016, Part 1 Section 3).

We don't need to worry about who, if anyone, is right in this debate. The debate is significant because it underlines that concern for the welfare of wild animals acts as a common denominator in the environmental community— one *must* be seen as pro-wildlife. Additionally, the debate highlights the fact that a nonanthropocentric concern for wild animals is seen as a moral reason to support conservation, with the implicit assumption that anthropocentrism is, by contrast, base, strictly economic, and sub-moral. Those who promote conservation of wild places by invoking the survival and welfare of wild animals believe themselves to be on righteous and morally uncomplicated ground. The following section will explain why they believe this is so; the section after that will argue that they are wrong.

THE ARGUMENT FROM WELFARE

An uncontroversial version of the AFW begins as follows:[3]

> AFW-1: If a being can subjectively feel, experience, and perceive, then it has the capacity for welfare, and has an interest in its own welfare. In other words, sentient beings can fare well or fare poorly, whereas a nonsentient being, like a rock, cannot. (We don't worry about the welfare of rocks because rocks can't fare well.)

> AFW-2: Sentience is a sufficient though not a necessary condition for moral considerability, i.e., for being the sort of entities that deserve moral consideration in our interactions with them. ('Sentience' stands here for the capacity to experience pleasure and pain, along with the capacity to have sensations.)

One of the triumphs of twentieth-century moral philosophy was to decisively establish that humans are not the only creatures worthy of moral consideration. To say that a being is morally considerable is to say "there is a moral claim that this being has on those who can recognize such claims" (Gruen 2010). Put another way, moral considerability is the quality a being must have in order for it to be morally wronged. Rocks are not morally considerable beings. If, walking down the road, I kick a rock out of my path I have not wronged the rock, and had I refrained from kicking it I would not have done right by the rock. Rocks just aren't the kind of beings that can be morally wronged. But if I kick my officemate Ed in the shin so that I can beat him to the fresh pot of coffee, I have done something wrong; I have morally wronged *him*. Ed is a human, and since humans are morally considerable I must recognize the moral claims he can make on me, in this instance the claim not to be harmed so that I can get the first cup of coffee.

For most of human history animals were considered, morally speaking, not much different from rocks. There may have been prudential reasons to treat or not treat them a certain way, but the reasons were not moral. Jeremy Bentham, creator of utilitarianism, made the first substantial plea for the moral considerability of animals over two hundred years ago, and his rightly famous statement is worth quoting at length:

> The day may come, when the rest of the animal creation may acquire those rights which never could have been withholden from them but by the hand of tyranny. The French have already discovered that the blackness of skin is no reason why a human being should be abandoned without redress to the caprice of a tormentor. It may come one day to be recognized, that the number of legs, the villosity of the skin, or the termination of the *os sacrum*, are reasons equally insufficient for abandoning a sensitive being to the same fate. . . . The question is not, Can they reason? nor, Can they talk? but, Can they suffer? Why should the law refuse its protection to any sensitive being? . . . The time will come when humanity will extend its mantle over everything which breathes. (Bentham 1996, 282n)

Bentham's idea is that there is no nonarbitrary, morally relevant reason to restrict the moral community (the set of all morally considerable beings) to humans. Just as we have come to reject moral discrimination on the basis of race and gender, so too should we reject moral discrimination purely on the basis of species. Peter Singer has popularized the term 'speciesism' to describe and condemn those who morally discriminate on the basis of species membership, just as 'racism' describes and condemns those who morally discriminate on the basis of race.

According to Bentham, a being is morally considerable if it has the capacity to suffer, though it is more common now to speak about sentience than about suffering. As noted above, "sentience" in this connection signifies an ability to feel, along with the ability to have experiences and perceive subjectively.

So then, if a being is sentient—regardless of race, gender or species—then it ought to be included in the moral community.[4]

The AFW accordingly continues as follows:

AFW-3: At least some nonhuman animals are sentient.

AFW-4: Therefore some nonhuman animals are morally considerable and ought to be included in the moral community.

Without making a comprehensive claim about the function or purpose of ethics and ethical behavior we can, at minimum, say:

AFW-5: A purpose of ethics is to promote concern for the welfare of morally considerable beings.

AFW-6: So, given AFW-4 and AFW-5, we have a moral reason to care about, or at least not disregard, the welfare of some nonhuman animals (or risk being 'speciesist').

The AFW concludes by making a connection between wilderness and animal welfare:

AFW-7: The destruction of wilderness inhibits nonhuman animal welfare, whereas wilderness preservation promotes nonhuman animal welfare.

Conclusion: Therefore, we have a moral reason to preserve the wilderness.

It bears reiterating that this argument is not the only argument for wilderness preservation. But anyone who has received a fundraising letter from the National Wildlife Federation or been stopped on the street by a Greenpeace volunteer knows that some version of the AFW—i.e., some appeal based on the welfare of wildlife—is standard practice. And even when other, anthropocentric reasons such as resource conservation or the economic boons of a green economy are presented, it is made clear that the *moral* reason to protect the wilderness is not because it is good for humans, but because it is good for all the other creatures whose welfare we ought to take into account.

A particular fundraising letter from the National Wildlife Federation exemplifies the strategy of the AFW. After explaining with words and pictures that polar bears are suffering due to human activity, the author writes: "That's why the single most important message I can deliver to you today isn't about polar bears at all. It's about you and your values. And one of the most effective ways you can show your values, and help imperiled wildlife like polar bears to survive, is by joining the National Wildlife Federation today!" (O'Mara

2016). The message is clear: for those of us with the right values, the welfare of polar bears (which starts with survival) should matter; hence, the preservation of wilderness should matter.

THE OBJECTION FROM WELFARE

The Objection from Welfare (OFW) agrees with the AFW on several points. It agrees that sentience is a sufficient condition for moral considerability; it agrees that some animals are sentient, thus morally considerable; and it agrees that animal welfare ought to matter. Yet the OFW stops short of endorsing the conclusion that concern for animal welfare goes hand in hand with a desire for wilderness preservation. The reason for this is that the OFW disputes AFW-7, the assertion that the destruction of wilderness inhibits animal welfare and that wilderness preservation promotes animal welfare.

The biological, ecological, and scientific facts on which the OFW is based should not be controversial. It is the argument and conclusion drawn from these facts that may spark controversy. While arguments resembling the OFW have been rare in the philosophical literature, they are not without precedent and are gaining prominence. In formalizing and presenting the OFW, I primarily draw on the work of Mark Sagoff and Jefferson McMahan (Sagoff 1984 and McMahan 2015).[5]

The argument for the OFW runs as follows:

OFW-1: At least some nonhuman animals are sentient.

OFW-2: Sentience is a sufficient condition for inclusion in the moral community.

OFW-3: We should have concern for the welfare of morally considerable beings.

OFW-4: Therefore (from 1–3) we should have concern for the welfare of at least some nonhuman animals.

OFW-5: Reducing non-beneficial, unjust, unchosen suffering promotes welfare.

Let me explain why I qualify the suffering to be reduced as non-beneficial, unjust, and unchosen.

Non-beneficial suffering means suffering that does ultimately promote the welfare of a morally considerable being. Many things that are ultimately good for us involve suffering to one degree or another: exercise, education, trips to the dentist, chemotherapy, psychotherapy. This is beneficial suffering. Non-beneficial suffering is suffering without an intended or reasonably likely positive effect on a being's welfare. By adding the qualification "unjust," I mean to avoid cases in which suffering is non-beneficial yet may still be permissible. An example might be a just fine imposed for a parking violation or, more seriously, a just prison sentence that results in some manner of suffering. The qualification "unchosen" is included to avoid cases in which an autonomous being knowingly exercises freedom to inflict some form of non-beneficial suffering on herself. It may be that, in the case of humans, the value of autonomy occasionally supersedes the value of happiness: think of the savage in *Brave New World* demanding the right to be unhappy. Perhaps some of us would rather freely lead ourselves into suffering than be forcefully led away from it.[6]

> OFW-6: We have a *pro tanto* moral reason to reduce non-beneficial, unjust, unchosen suffering if we can.
>
> OFW-7: Wilderness entails vast amounts of non-beneficial, unjust, unchosen suffering on the part of morally considerable beings in the wilderness (in other words, a wilderness negatively impacts the welfare of wildlife living in it).
>
> OFW-8: At least some of the suffering in the wilderness is unnecessary and could be eliminated through human intervention.
>
> Conclusion: Concern about the welfare of morally considerable nonhuman animals sometimes provides a *pro tanto* reason to intervene in the natural world such that we diminish or eliminate wilderness conditions.

The heart of the argument is OFW-3: the belief that life in the wilderness entails incalculable amounts of suffering for the vast majority of wildlife, especially those who are not top predators (though they are hardly immune). A life in the wild is one overwhelmingly characterized by fear, predation, stress, disease, parasitism, exposure, hunger, infanticide, cannibalism, and early death. In Mark Sagoff's memorable summation: "Mother Nature is so cruel to her children she makes Frank Perdue look like a saint" (Sagoff 1984, 303). Before saying anything about the goodness or badness of this state of affairs, we must first recognize that it *is* the state of affairs in the wilderness.

The fact that wild nature entails unbelievable suffering for millions upon millions of sentient organisms, generation after generation, has not previously gone unnoticed. In the nineteenth century, Arthur Schopenhauer used the endless suffering of nature to defend his pessimistic view that the world contains more unhappiness than happiness (Schopenhauer 1970, 42), while scientists like Charles Darwin and Charles Lyell struggled mightily to square the magnitude of natural suffering with their desire to believe in a benevolent God (Gould 1982). More recently, Richard Dawkins, one of Darwin's intellectual descendants (and not coincidently a fervent atheist), has reaffirmed the unpleasant truth:

> The total amount of suffering per year in the natural world is beyond all decent contemplation. During the minute that it takes me to compose this sentence, thousands of animals are being eaten alive, many others are running for their lives, whimpering with fear, others are slowly being devoured from within by rasping parasites, thousands of all kinds are dying of starvation, thirst, and disease. (Dawkins 1995, 133)

In considering the lot of wild animals, environmental philosopher Eugene Hargrove concludes:

> Their lives are extremely hazardous. Under natural conditions, they may be killed or eaten at almost any time. The only way to be reasonably sure that any particular animals will have an opportunity to live out a full life span is to remove them from their natural habitat and place them in an artificial environment—such as a zoo or a park—where they are safe from predation and other hazards. Medical care, comparable to that provided for human beings, is also a must. (Hargrove 1989, 128)

Like Sagoff, Hargrove is not intending to endorse anything resembling the OFW. This is a relevant point, as one cannot claim that their assessment of animal welfare is self-serving. They are simply reporting what any honest observer of nature must.

Many animals are nonsentient (e.g., oysters) in which case they are not included in the AFW or OFW. But many nonhuman animals *are* sentient. While I tend to believe that the claim that wild animal populations experience incredible, incalculable suffering is obvious and undeniable (again, it is only the moral implication of this fact that should be debatable), a couple of illustrations may help those who can't shake a benign, Disneyesque view of the natural world. Take the case of predation:

> When a lioness sinks her scimitar talons into the zebra's rump, the startled animal lets out a loud bellow as its body hits the ground. An instant later the lioness releases her claws from its buttocks and sinks her teeth into the zebra's throat, choking off the sound of terror. Her canine teeth are long and sharp, but an animal as large as a zebra has a massive neck, with a thick layer of muscle beneath the skin, so although the teeth puncture the hide they are too short to reach any major blood vessels. She must therefore kill the zebra by asphyxiation, clamping her powerful jaws around its trachea. . . . The zebra's death throes will last five or six minutes. (McGowan 1997, 12–13)

Parasitism provides another vivid example of animal misery. Wild animals are hundreds of times more likely to suffer from ectoparasites and endoparasites than non-wild animals. From birth to death they have ticks and worms attacking their eyes, mouth, skin, stomach, genitals, and immune system. Why do we seek to keep ourselves and the animals we care about free from harmful parasites? Because we know that the host animal suffers greatly, and we at least implicitly recognize the intrinsic badness of suffering. We cannot reasonably think wild animals don't suffer as well.

Perhaps most significant is the fact that the vast majority of wild animals die very young. Not only do their abbreviated lives tend to include more suffering than flourishing, and not only are their deaths typically wretched and violent, but early death has an opportunity cost: it rules out the possibility for that particular animal of enjoying whatever it is that makes its life worth living. The overwhelming majority of animals born in the wild will die before their first birthday. "If the wild animal understood the conditions into which it is born," asks Sagoff, "what would it think? It might reasonably prefer to be raised on a farm where the chances of survival for a year or more would be good, and to escape from the wild, where the chances are negligible"—though admittedly not the factory farm (Sagoff 1984, 303).

Evolutionary biologist Christie Wilcox bolsters Sagoff's suggestion. "We have no evidence whatsoever," she writes, "that wild animals are, in any way, happier than domesticated ones which are treated well" (Wilcox 2011, Section 3). In fact, it is quite the opposite. Veterinarians understand animal welfare (or happiness) to include safe access to food and water, freedom from stress, fear, and suffering, and the ability to engage in natural behaviors and live out the natural course of a life. By this metric, domesticated and semidomesticated animals usually fare far better than their wild counterparts.

This is particularly so in the case of stress. Wild animals have much higher levels of the stress hormone cortisol than domesticated animals. To give a particular example, concentrations of serum epinephrine and norepinephrine, two other stress hormones, are four times lower in domesticated guinea pigs than wild guinea pigs (ibid., section 3). The reason for the difference is clear. Life in the wild is perilous at every moment. A relaxed, placid guinea pig wouldn't be long for this world. In the wild, avoiding early death and securing enough food to live long enough to reproduce necessitates a life predominated by fear and stress. A being that must live such a life just to survive can hardly be said to be faring well. A human living such a life would be a subject of pity; a community of humans living such lives would constitute a crisis; and an entire human system predicated on this state of affairs repeating itself in a never-ending cycle would be a moral nightmare.

At least part of what would make such a life or community or system so bad would be the endless, undeserved, unchosen suffering to which sentient, morally considerable beings were being subjected. But many animals are sentient. Their suffering is no less real and no less morally considerable simply because they don't belong to the species *humanus*. They may suffer less than humans in certain ways; for example, the complexity of human psychology can make the effects of fear and stress more painful and enduring for us than what most animals experience (McMahan 2015, 281). But even conceding that human beings may be capable of greater suffering than animals, we cannot deny the magnitude of the animal suffering such as it is.

To summarize the OFW: the magnitude and constancy of undeserved, unchosen, non-beneficial suffering that exists in the wilderness gives us a strong moral reason to oppose this state of affairs. It remains unclear what an individual or a society impressed by the OFW could do to ameliorate the situation. My suspicion is that, at present, very little ought to be attempted.[7] But this is not a mark against the OFW. The first task of moral philosophy is to ask questions and acquire a body of moral knowledge. We first have to determine, based on the best available arguments, whether we morally ought to take a certain course of action. Only once this is done does the task become how to make it happen. Take the case of slavery. The first and most important step toward abolition was to demonstrate the moral impermissibility of slavery. Only once this was firmly established was it necessary to devise means of dismantling the institution.

Nevertheless, some early suggestions on how we might reduce suffering in the wilderness have been made. Suggestions include providing medical care for sick or wounded animals, rescuing animals imperiled by natural disasters, limiting populations with birth control, and altering or removing (or refraining from reintroducing) top predators (see McMahan 2015, Pearce 2015, Sagoff 1984, Cowen 2003, Horta 2010, and Reese 2015). The last two suggestions usually provoke incredulity, sometimes anger. I will say more about them in the next section. For now, the salient point is this: if we determine that the moral reasons to intervene in wilderness are stronger than the moral reasons not to intervene, then we must begin finding ways to make this intervention practical, however scientifically, technically, and politically challenging it appears at the present time.

CHALLENGING THE OFW

It is hard to imagine environmentalists of any ideological persuasion endorsing the OFW, as the OFW gives one a strong moral reason to intervene in the natural world and disrupt, possibly dismantle, wilderness.[8] Still, many do endorse some version of the AFW, and anyone who is inclined to endorse the

AFW must dispute the conclusion of the OFW. There are four ways to do so, namely, by disputing

1. the factual claims in question,
2. the practicality,
3. the values, or
4. the logic.

This section considers and responds to 1–4 in turn.

Disputing the Factual Claims

The OFW fails if animals do not really suffer in the wild. But there is a preponderance of evidence (common sense and scientific) to make us believe that wild animals do suffer, and that they suffer greatly. One cannot plausibly reject the OFW by claiming that wild animals do not suffer, or do not suffer much. The factual claims made by the OFW are beyond dispute, rendering moot this first strategy of contesting it.[9]

Disputing the Practicality

This objection is usually the primary objection made against the OFW, and at first blush the most damaging. If it is impossible to lessen the suffering of wild animals through human intervention without necessarily causing an equivalent or greater amount of suffering, then we must reject the OFW. According to McMahan, the "commonest objection" to ending predation through deliberate intervention is that "the complexity of any major ecosystem so far surpasses our understanding that an attempt to eliminate predators within it . . . would have unpredictable and potentially catastrophic ramifications throughout the system" (McMahan 2015, 274). We can imagine a Malthusian nightmare in which reduced predation and disease causes populations to explode, thus creating a situation in which suffering increases through starvation and increased competition for scarce resources. If the welfare of sentient wild animals necessarily depends on the presence of top predators, disease, etc., then no wild animal is benefited if and when top predators, disease, etc. are removed.

McMahan, who does endorse a narrow version of the OFW aimed at eliminating predation, has a cogent response. It is true, for example, that simply eliminating top predators without taking any other action would likely decrease rather than increase animal welfare, not least of all for the predators being eliminated. But this observation only implies that the removal of predators must be done in the right way, not that it shouldn't be done. McMahan proposes that if and when predators are removed from an ecosystem, some kind of nonsurgical selective sterilization of prey could be used to maintain a healthy population of herbivores. He also suggests that germline genetic modification could eventually be used to gradually transform predatory carnivores into herbivores. In principle, there is no reason why we could not find a way to maintain healthy ecosystems while also increasing animal welfare through the elimination of disease, predation, and early death. Human beings have long been engaged in just such an enterprise on behalf of our own welfare. While we are now realizing that there are limits to how much we can safely alter the state of nature without it becoming counterproductive to present or future generations, no one seriously maintains that the fate of human beings would be better if we remained permanently in the wild, subject to the amoral laws of evolution by means of natural selection, without any of the trappings of culture or civilization.

Many will balk at the idea that we could ever have the scientific knowledge or technological prowess necessary to safely follow McMahan's proposal. But this is a shortsighted thinking. The history of science and technology teaches that today's science fiction frequently becomes just plain science a few decades, centuries, or millennia down the road.

> What may now seem forever impossible may yield to the advance of science in a surprisingly short time—as happened when Rutherford, the first scientist to split the atom, who announced in 1933 that anyone who claimed that atomic fission could be a source of power talking "moonshine." Unless we use Rutherford's discovery or others like it to destroy ourselves first, we will almost certainly be able eventually to eliminate predation while preserving the stability and harmony of ecosystems. (ibid., 274)

Three thousand years ago, the notion of a metal tube carrying people to the moon would have seemed madness. Three hundred years ago the belief that tiny creatures inhabit our blood and can make us ill was less plausible than witchcraft. And just three decades ago the idea that we could put a human embryo in a dish, tinker with it, and engineer a new kind of person was more of a fantasy than a legitimate research project. When something is logically possible and morally desirable, those who bet against it becoming practically achievable usually turn out to be wrong. The moral and political will to change a state of affairs is all it takes to make fantastic ideas scientifically, technologically, and economically feasible.

The objection based on practicality is implicit in AFW-4, which states that the destruction of wilderness negatively impacts animal welfare. We are so used to human interference in or destruction of wilderness being shortsighted, economically motivated, and ecologically disastrous that it is challenging to conceive of impacting wilderness in other ways. If one only imagines strip mining, clear-cutting, and the anthropogenic bleaching of coral reefs, then yes, the destruction of wilderness is inimical to animal welfare. But if one imagines germline genetic modification to phase out predation (or one of the other tentative suggestions), the matter is not so simple. Wilderness is diminished or destroyed when humans significantly alter nature. But human intervention in nature can take many forms: some very bad for other morally considerable, some potentially good. To significantly intervene in nature is to necessarily diminish or destroy wilderness, but that does mean that the morally considerable beings inhabiting and partially constituting wilderness must be harmed in the process.

A different kind of practical objection questions whether we have the resources to concern ourselves with the welfare of wildlife when we cannot adequately protect the welfare of all human beings. Given our limited time and resources, surely we need to focus on poverty, war, and healthcare rather than helping stressed-out guinea pigs.

This objection is probably true so far as it goes. But there are three responses. First, it does not obviate the *pro tanto* moral reason we have to reduce suffering and promote animal welfare. It merely (though correctly, I think) points out that at present we probably have more pressing moral projects with which to engage, and that these other projects currently have a higher probability of success. Second, if we take this objection to be decisive, we would have a hard time justifying our engagement in any moral project so long as a more important moral project exists that makes a stronger claim on our time and resources. The fight for fair pay in the workplace regardless of gender seems to me like an important cause, but I do not think it is more important than the fight to end human trafficking. Still, I do not chastise people who put their resources into the struggle for wage fairness rather than the struggle to end human trafficking. Unless one is prepared to criticize everyone who engages in a moral cause that is not the most immediately pressing, it seems unfair to criticize the OFW on the grounds that it may not be the most important ethical problem we face (ibid., 290–91). The third response is that given the scope and scale of suffering that occurs in the wild, proponents of the OFW could plausibly respond that the suffering of wild animals constitutes as great a moral crisis as any other. Very likely it is far greater (ibid., 291).[10]

Disputing the Values

Even if we accept the facts and the potential practicality of the OFW, we might still question the values on which it is based. In other words, just because animals suffer, and just because we could potentially reduce their suffering, why should we think that the suffering of wild animals is, morally speaking, bad? As Dawkins reminds us:

> In a universe of electrons and selfish genes, blind physical forces and genetic replication, some people are going to get hurt, other people are going to get lucky, and you won't find any rhyme or reason in it, nor any justice. The universe that we observe has precisely the properties we should expect if there is, at bottom, no design, no purpose, no evil, no good, nothing but pitiless indifference. (Dawkins 1995, 133)

Right and wrong, good and bad, virtue and vice—these are features of the human world, not wilderness. In the wild nothing is good or bad—it just is. Why, then, should we be morally concerned about suffering in an amoral sphere?

This objection makes two mistakes. First, it wrongly affirms the following conditional: *if animal suffering isn't a moral issue for animals or nature or the universe, then it can't be a moral issue for human beings.* Moral agents are beings capable of understanding and acting upon moral norms such that we can hold the beings morally responsible for their actions. Animals (and nature, and the universe) are not moral agents. But just because something is not a moral agent doesn't mean that it is not a moral patient. A moral patient is a being toward whom a moral agent can have moral responsibility. For example, we do not regard human infants as moral agents. We do not (or should not) morally blame them for disturbing our sleep, flinging mashed peas, or pulling the cat's tail. But we do regard infants as moral patients, that is, we regard them as beings to whom moral agents have a moral responsibility. And the reason this is the case is not solely because they are members of our species.

Imagine you are in the grocery store and you see an infant reach out and knock a box of cereal off the shelf. The infant's parent slaps him hard across the face. Why is this wrong? Even though there are issues of rights, laws, and parental duties, the primary reason we think this action is morally wrong is because it harms the child. Despite not yet having the capacity to commit moral wrongs, the infant certainly has capacity to suffer them. And even if the infant never develops into a moral agent (suppose it suffers severe brain damage and remains, mentally, an infant all its life) we would still consider it impermissible to treat him as anything less than a morally considerable being.

Even if the animal world contains no moral agents, it surely contains moral patients. The fact that morality and justice are anthropo*genic* is no reason to think they ought to be anthropo*centric*. Much environmental ethics and concern for animal liberation are premised on expanding the moral community to include nonhuman animals and the natural world. If we have no business inserting our human moral knowledge into the amoral world of nature, then ethics should be necessarily and unapologetically anthropocentric.

The second mistake this objection makes is that it fails to realize that suffering is intrinsically bad even if no one is morally responsible for it. Since suffering occurs in the wild, badness exists in the wild. No being, moral or amoral, is responsible for volcanoes and earthquakes, yet the suffering and early death they cause are bad. And it makes no difference that the lion is not morally responsible to the zebra. The badness of the suffering is independent of any moral ascription of responsibility. Dawkins is right to say that there is no justice in nature, but this does not mean there is no badness in nature. The zebra, for its part, does not care whether the suffering comes from an amoral lion or an immoral person. All that matters from the zebra's point of view is the suffering because it is the suffering itself, not the violation of some moral responsibility, which decreases the zebra's welfare.

Disputing the Logic

This objection is more promising than the previous three. It asks why the recognition that wild animals suffer and are morally considerable logically entails that we ought to intervene on their behalf. It might be that we have a duty of non-maleficence toward wild animals, but no duty of beneficence. What this distinction means is that, while we might be morally required to refrain from harming wild animals, we have no duty to actively improve their lives. If this were true, it would be wrong for us to clear-cut a forest because it would harm animals but it would not be wrong of us to leave the forest as we find it, regardless of the predation, disease, suffering, and early death such noninterference entails. The merit of this objection depends on whether you think we have positive moral duties to help animals when the cost to ourselves is minimal or merely negative moral duties to avoid causing harm to animals.

Disputes over the priority, difference betweeen, and relative importance of duties of beneficence and non-maleficence run deep in the history of moral philosophy. I cannot here settle those disputes and I make no pretense of doing so; fortunately, I do I think I need to. The OFW does not need to support a strict duty of beneficence (which I admit it does not do). All it must do is demonstrate that we have a *pro tanto* moral reason to oppose non-beneficial, unchosen, undeserved suffering. McMahan is characteristically illuminating on this point:

> Most people who read this [McMahan's] chapter will recognize a moral reason to avoid causing animals to suffer if can we do so without cost, and that this is because suffering is intrinsically bad for those that experience it. . . . Most of

us believe, rightly in my view, that our moral reason not to cause suffering is in general stronger than our reason to prevent it from occurring—for example, to prevent someone or something else from causing it. . . . But that is compatible with our having a strong reason to prevent suffering in animals for which we would be in no way responsible when we can do so at little or no cost to ourselves. (McMahan 2015, 273)

Absent a strict moral duty of beneficence toward the natural world such that we are morally obligated to intervene, the OFW still gives us a compelling moral reason to try to improve the welfare of our fellow sentient beings even if we follow McMahan in adding the caveat that this reason becomes operative only when it comes at little or no cost to ourselves.

The idea of a compelling moral reason that may still fall short of an obligation is easily illustrated with a now conventional anthropocentric analogy (familiar no doubt to those who have taken or taught an introductory course in ethics). Let's say I have twenty dollars that I don't need to meet any of my basic needs. I see an advert from Save the Children telling me that a $20 donation will provide medical care for a child who will otherwise die. I put in my due diligence and conclude that the advert's claim is reliable. Now, whether or not I have an absolute moral duty to send twenty dollars to Save the Children, I certainly have a strong moral reason to do so, and doing so would surely be a good for the child. Similarly, those who argue that we don't have a duty to intervene in nature when doing so can prevent more harm than it causes, and can be done at little or no cost to us, need to explain why we *shouldn't* intervene. To put it another way, they need to explain why the moral reason not to intervene is stronger than the moral reason to intervene.[11]

CONCLUSION

The AFW is a favored tool in the struggle for wilderness preservation because it rightly recognizes the moral considerability of wild animals. In doing so, it gives wilderness defenders a nonanthropocentric reason, and thus supposedly a moral reason, to preserve the wilderness. Whereas arguments for wilderness preservation that rely on human wants and needs can be dismissed by those who do not share these wants and needs (or who think artificial environments can satisfy them just as well), the AFW focuses on the welfare of beings that are unable to participate in the discussion yet are disproportionately adversely affected by the conclusions.

Unfortunately, the OFW demonstrates that the AFW, according to its own principles, must be committed to eradicating wilderness conditions if and when it would increase animal welfare without causing an equivalent or greater decrease in welfare for other morally considerable beings. Since none of the objections to the OFW are insurmountable, anyone who supports the AFW but rejects the OFW will have to revise or abandon one or more of its premises and the moral commitments on which they are based. Furthermore, anyone who desires the preservation of wilderness yet rejects both the AFW and OFW will have to explain why the existence of the wilderness *qua* wilderness is more valuable than the alleviation of the suffering of incalculable millions of sentient creatures.

Those persuaded by the OFW must still acknowledge (as Singer, McMahan and others do) that at present any attempt at large-scale intervention on behalf of wild animals is likely to be counterproductive. The system is too complex and the present state of our ecological knowledge too limited for us to have a reasonable chance at increasing welfare without causing greater harm. Most moral philosophers agree that, however strong the duty to intervene may be, the duty to avoid causing harm will always take primacy: beneficence begins with nonmaleficence. But again, nonintervention on the grounds of nonmaleficence is pegged to the current state of our scientific knowledge and technological capacities. Changes in what we know and what we can do may influence how we ought to act.

The lovers and defenders of wilderness ought to examine the reasons they have for loving and defending it.[12] If the reasons are distinct from issues of animal welfare, they need to ask whether these reasons morally trump the unremitting suffering and early death of innumerable morally considerable creatures. If the reasons invoke animal welfare as a, or even as the, primary moral justification, then they will need to start considering what, if anything, would be wrong with a world in which suffering is reduced and welfare is increased but no areas of land or sea largely untouched by the hand of man remain to be seen.

There is another, more pointed, lesson to be drawn that concerns the intramural fighting between factions within the conservation community, particularly scientists and policy experts. The disagreement between "traditional" and "new" conservation, discussed at the start of this chapter, shows how entrenched and divisive these disputes become. We also saw the alacrity with which participants in conservation debates resort to moral language and moral condemnation. This strategy is not *prima facie* unreasonable. If you can paint your opponent as not just wrong but *morally* wrong, you've landed a heavy blow.

Yet the considerable danger of this strategy is twofold. First, moral attacks have the tendency to alienate rather than engage one's opponent. As a method of academic dialogue or policy discussion it is ineffective at best, inflammatory at worst. Second, we know so little about the moral problems associated with wilderness preservation that blanket ascriptions of right and wrong, moral and immoral, seem unjustified. Environmental ethics, which is barely fifty years old, remains in its intellectual infancy. Our ignorance vastly outstrips our understanding; we are still coming to grips with the problems let alone confident in the solutions. This is not a reason for environmental quietism or for the abdication of environmental responsibility, but it is a reason for intellectual caution and moral humility.

The traditional view of environmental ethics has been that anthropocentric arguments imperil wilderness while nonanthropocentric arguments can keep it safe. What this chapter has shown is that there is a cogent nonanthropocentric position that puts the future of wilderness in jeopardy by providing strong moral reasons against the maintenance of wilderness conditions. I accept that the arguments presented in this chapter are counterintuitive. But that's the point. By believing the moral issues of wilderness to be simpler than they are, we may find ourselves logically committed to destroying what we meant to protect. Lean too hard on the moral dimension of a dispute in a way that casts aspersion and we are likely to alienate our interlocutor; lean too hard on a moral dimension of an issue about which we still know very little, and we may alienate ourselves from the very position we intended to hold. Neither anthropocentric nor nonanthropocentric proponents have a monopoly on the moral high ground. We are all trudging through the ethical muck together. Given the uncertainly, nothing is gained when those directly involved in environmental action make hasty declarations of moral superiority.

NOTES

1. To be sure, Muir and Pinchot are figures of *American* environmentalism. Yet the conservationist/preservationist divide that they embodied knows no national bounds.

2. Continued existence is a necessary condition for faring well. Thus any focus on "saving" wildlife is a concern for their welfare in the most basic form.

3. The literature on animal welfare and animal rights is vast (leaving alone the literature on welfare and rights *tout court*), and there is continuing debate over the nature of animal welfare and the nature of our duties toward nonhuman creatures. I cannot settle these debates here. My strategy is to use what I consider a minimal, and now relatively uncontroversial, conception of animal welfare based in the sentientist, utilitarian views most famously, though not exclusively, expressed by Peter Singer (Singer 1990). I am not discounting a rights-based approach such as that offered by Tom Regan (Regan 1983), and I think the AFW and OFW could be couched in terms of rights. But the case for animal rights (indeed, the case for rights in general) is more difficult to defend, and more controversial, than an ethic based on sentientism and suffering. In short: it is easier to get agreement that animals suffer than it is to get agreement that animals have rights. Moreover, even if animals do have rights, their capacity for suffering remains an important, if not the most important, moral

consideration. And since all that is needed for the present argument is to acknowledge that animals suffer, that is all I intend to do.

4. Here some may object that I have unfairly excluded nonsentient plants and animals from the moral community. A biocentrist like Kenneth Goodpaster (Goodpaster 1978) would argue that this exclusion is no less arbitrary than the exclusion of nonhuman sentient creatures that Bentham and Singer oppose. Goodpaster may point out that nonsentient living beings still have ends and goods of their own that can be furthered or thwarted. I have two reasons for not taking up the issue of biocentrism here, though I will in chapter 3. First, acknowledging the moral considerability of nonsentient life would not damage the argument of this chapter—if anything, it would strengthen it. While I cannot say that nonsentient life suffers in the wild, it is certainly vulnerable to whatever sort of badness biocentrists think applies—early death, competition for scarce resources, the pitiless roulette wheel of natural selection. Life for an oyster or fern under wilderness conditions is no less perilous than life for a chipmunk. But while adopting a biocentric view may help my position, I do not endorse it because I not to think it is possible to establish intrinsic moral considerability for nonsentient beings. I follow Dale Jamieson's, Bernard Williams's, and Jana Thompson's arguments that a being must be capable of having experiences (and thus be sentient) in order to have interests in a morally relevant sense. Without the capacity for experiences, as Jamieson notes, nothing that happens to a being can matter to it: "For this reason, identifying sentience as the criterion for moral considerability is not arbitrary" (Jamieson 2008, 147). "What is essential for having interests is that it matter to the being what happens to her. This is what is true of humans and many other animals, and what is not true of plants" (ibid., 148). Williams and Thompson make similar claims in dismissing the appeals of ecocentrists that even species and ecosystems have interests, rights, and welfare (See Williams 1994 and Thompson 1990).

5. For additional, excellent discussions of wild animal welfare, see: Johannsen 2021a and 2021b; Delon and Purves 2018; Horta 2018 and 2017; Palmer 2018; Kymlicka and Donaldson 2014.

6. Jean Kazez helpfully discusses the potential irreducibility of competing goods like happiness and autonomy. See Kazez 2007, 61–80.

7. Eugene Hargrove uses the term 'therapeutic nihilism' to denote the human attempt to help or save wildlife and wilderness by simply leaving it alone. It is a version of Barry Commoner's third law of ecology: "Nature knows best." While nature most certainly does not know best (it knows nothing) I agree that *at the present moment* a massive reduction in human meddling may be an optimal strategy for those concerned about the welfare for wildlife and wilderness. See Hargrove 1989, 137–61 and Commoner 1971.

8. As noted, in the rare instances where something like the OFW appears in the literature, it is heretical. McMahan's article, "The Moral Problem of Predation," drew the ire of some ecologists and environmental philosophers. They accused him of misunderstanding basic facts about biology and ecology and of trying to replace nature's values with his own. Ecologist Paul Falkowski tells McMahan: "it is clear you have either never taken a course in ecology and evolution, or forgot the message" (quoted in ibid., 287). But such criticisms are a category mistake. McMahan makes no claims

at all about biology, ecology, or evolution; he is making a moral claim, and "whether we have a moral reason to prevent the suffering of animals is not an ecological issue" (ibid., 287).

9. Any attempt to argue that wild animals are unable to suffer, i.e., that they are not sentient, is as damaging for the AFW as it is for the OFW. It's not possible to protest deforestation or development by appealing to the welfare of animals if you've argued that animals aren't sentient.

10. McMahan's elucidation of the moral problem of predation and his analysis of the objections against it is brilliant. His work is a model of philosophical clarity. Anyone interested in the moral issue of predation, or animal welfare more generally, should read his work.

11. It is hard to say where this type of analogy first appeared or who first used it, but a famous version of it appears in Peter Unger's *Living High and Letting Die*. It has subsequently been used in various forms by countless commentators. See: Unger, Peter. 1996. *Living High & Letting Die: Our Illusion of Innocence*. Oxford: Oxford University Press.

12. Here I must acknowledge that I, like every other participant in the debate, am a lover of wilderness. It would be of enormous help to environmental philosophy if at least some environmental philosophers were not also nature lovers and environmental activists. Philosophers are trained to take a skeptical stance and consider all arguments, but the danger for confirmation bias in this field is overwhelming.

Chapter Three

Intrinsic Value and Nonanthropocentrism

Chapter 2 argued that the OFW gives a *pro tanto* reason to question the morality of wilderness preservation. The argument is unexpected given that appeals to animal welfare are often put forth in defense of wilderness preservation. To be sure, if one imagines a disjunction in which we either leave wilderness as it is or interfere in some ecologically disastrous way for the purpose of extracting oil or building vacation homes, then the preservation of wilderness clearly would advance the cause of animal welfare. But no such disjunction is necessary. There is no reason why diminishment or destruction of wilderness through thoughtful augmentation must be disastrous, vulgar, and inimical to the welfare of morally considering beings. At minimum, moral deliberation is required once this point is acknowledged.

It is already within our power to deliberately interfere with wilderness to ameliorate some of the suffering wilderness entails. Let us then imagine a future in which two things become possible. First, it becomes possible to alleviate the non-beneficial, unchosen, undeserved suffering on a scale such that, once accomplished, wilderness will only exist to a very small degree; human fingerprints, so to speak, will be on everything and will be *intentionally* on everything. Second, it becomes possible to do this without the subsequent global environmental collapse often associated with human intervention in the natural world. Tropical forests will not whither; oceans will not acidify; the atmosphere will not be made toxic. In sum, imagine a future in which it is possible to bring about the end of wilderness without imperiling the welfare of present or future human and nonhuman animals. In such a state of affairs, what defense of wilderness would be possible? What reason, if any, could be mustered against the OFW such that even in this a hypothetical future, a cogent defense of wilderness would be forthcoming?

If advocates of wilderness remain intent on mounting a defense of wilderness, I submit they can do so only by successfully ascribing a certain value to wilderness. The value of diminishing or eliminating wilderness (in the right way, at the right time, to the right extent) could, if nothing else, be the value of the reduction in non-beneficial, unchosen, undeserved suffering for incalculable millions of morally considerable beings. A satisfactory defense of wilderness does not necessarily require the refutation of the OFW. But it does require an ascription of value to wilderness that can generate at least as strong a reason to support wilderness as the reason the OFW generates to oppose it. To this end, chapter 3 addresses the issue of value in general so that we will be in position to assess the value of wilderness and consider the merit of arguments put forth in its defense, tasks which are the subject of chapters 4 and 5.

There are six parts to this consideration. The first reviews the centrality that the concepts of intrinsic value and anthropocentrism have had, and continue to have, for environmental ethics. The second discusses four senses of intrinsic value and what it would mean for wilderness to have intrinsic value in each sense. The third examines the concept of anthropocentrism and three forms of nonanthropocentrism prominent in environmental ethics. The fourth presents reasons why, at best, only two senses of intrinsic value should have relevance to the wilderness debate. The fifth links the debate over of intrinsic value to the debate over anthropocentricism, and then provides reasons for thinking that some form of sentientism is the only viable form of nonanthropocentrism. The final part explains why the other nonanthropocentric positions dominant in environmental ethics—biocentrism and ecocentrism—would not, even if defensible, necessarily lead to arguments in defense of wilderness *qua* wilderness as they are commonly supposed to do. Instead, if cogent, biocentrism and ecocentrism would strengthen the OFW. No ascription of moral considerability to nonhuman organisms or ecosystems is going to produce a defense of wilderness *qua* wilderness.

INTRINSIC VALUE, ANTHROPOCENTRISM, AND ENVIRONMENTAL ETHICS

In 1973 Richard Routley presented a paper to the Fifteenth World Congress of Philosophy in Sofia, Bulgaria titled: "Is there a need for a new, an environmental, ethic?" (Routley 1973). He answered in the affirmative. His thesis was that it was not possible to generate moral arguments to protect the nonhuman, natural world using the tools of traditional, chauvinistic, anthropocentric moral philosophy. He argued that a new, truly environmental ethic must recognize the nonanthropocentric, intrinsic value of nature. Routley's paper and thesis can be taken as the beginning of professional philosophy's involvement with environmental issues

While the appropriate answer to Routley's question remains contentious, the question's impact on environmental philosophy is undeniable. Jamieson calls it "the galvanizing question for environmental ethics" such that "the search for a new, environmental ethics had been central to the development of the field" (Jamieson 2008, 68). The search for this new ethic, which is essentially an exercise in value theory, has focused on two related concepts: intrinsic value and nonanthropocentrism.

Overwhelmingly, and for reasons that will become clear, environmental ethicists have wanted to defend a nonanthropocentric ethic, and to do this they have felt the need to establish some sort of intrinsic value for nature.[1] As Jamieson puts it:

> For many philosophers [establishing an environmental ethic] involved developing a theory of intrinsic value that encompasses not just humanity and other sentient animals, but nature itself. . . . They wanted this new environmental ethics to be grounded in the nature of things, and not just an expression of the current, perhaps passing, concern for the environment. (Ibid., 68)

Anthony Weston draws attention to the fact that environmental philosopher Tom Regan defines "an environmental ethic as a view which attributes 'inherent goodness' to at least some nonhuman natural object, where 'inherent goodness' is an 'objective property' of objects which compels us to respect its bearers" (Weston 1985, 323). Bryan Norton observes that "the question of whether environmental ethics is distinctive is taken as equivalent to the question of whether an environmental ethic must reject anthropocentrism, the view that only humans are loci of fundamental value" (Norton 1984, 132). In considering the beings that make up the nonhuman natural world, John Benson asks:

> Should we value them, and be careful in our treatment of them, only because of the manifold ways in which they are useful to us, or do they, or some of them, have value which transcends and is independent of human interests? This is one of the most—perhaps the most—fundamental question in environmental ethics." (Benson 2000, 1)

And for Erazim Kohak, an environmental ethic must recognize that "nature in its integrity is not simply a reservoir of raw materials . . . the sense of nature as humans encounter it . . . is also moral, a presence of value" (Kohak 1984, 76).

Clearly concerns about intrinsic value and anthropocentrism have been hallmarks of environmental ethics since its inception. As a branch of environmental ethics, the same is true for wilderness ethics. Behind all arguments for or against the preservation of wilderness lie (a) some belief (though not always an argument) regarding the value of wilderness, (b) the meaning of intrinsic value, and (c) the question of the acceptability of anthropocentrism as a moral axis.

INTRINSIC VALUE

Intrinsic value, like wilderness, is a concept that tends to be understood and employed in a variety of ways. And as was the case with the idea of wilderness, the multifarious uses and meanings are sources of confusion and difficulty for debates in which intrinsic value plays a significant role.

There are at least four recognized types of intrinsic value we need to consider. It is vital that authors identify the type they have in mind given that much hangs on the type of intrinsic value one introduces. The import of the claim "the wilderness lacks intrinsic value" obviously turns on what "intrinsic value," in this instance, might mean. The aim of this section is to identify the four types of intrinsic value that have had some traction in environmental ethics debates.[2]

Intrinsic Value as Ultimate, Non-Instrumental Value

Intrinsic value in a first sense ("intrinsic value$_1$") is probably the most common sense of intrinsic value, and it is most easily understood as contrasting with instrumental value. A thing has value instrumentally if the benefit or good it provides is that of a means to some other end. Money is the paradigmatic example. Most of us value money, but we do not value coins and bills because we like round bits of metal and rectangular pieces of paper. We value money because we can use it to get at things that have non-instrumental value. If instrumental value is defined as that which is valuable only because it helps us get at other things that we value, intrinsic value$_1$ is defined as that which we considered valuable for itself, that for which things of instrumental value are simply a means to an end. I have an old hunting knife that belonged to my grandfather. Unlike money, and unlike the knives in my kitchen (which are mere means to cutting vegetables) my grandfather's knife is, for me, an end in itself. Using it, simply owning it, brings me satisfaction. As such, the knife has a kind of non-instrumental, ultimate value.

There is no consensus on what thing, or things, can have ultimate, non-instrumental value. Is it pleasure, or freedom, or God? Perhaps the Form of the Good? Can multiple things have ultimate value, or must all value reduce to a single source? These are important metaethical questions, but they need not concern us now. To claim that wilderness has intrinsic value$_1$ would be claim that wilderness is valued for itself, not as instrument or means that gains us access to some other valuable thing.

Intrinsic Value as Morally Considerable

Sometimes when we say that a thing has intrinsic value we mean that it has an independent moral status such that it deserves moral consideration. In chapter 2 we saw that sentience was a sufficient condition for moral considerability. Thus, we can say that sentient beings have intrinsic value in this second sense ("intrinsic value$_2$"). Any being that has intrinsic value$_2$ must figure in our moral deliberations for its own sake, and not only because it is or could be valuable to another member of the moral community.

Think again of my grandfather's knife. Using it, simply owning it, is a source of satisfaction for me. As such, I can say that the knife has intrinsic value$_1$. It is valuable for itself, not merely as a tool to perform some task for which any other knife would do just as well. But this does not make my grandfather's knife intrinsically valuable in the sense of morally considerable. The knife's value, such as it is, derives from the value I place in it. Because I value the knife, it would be wrong for others to mistreat it by leaving it to rust in the rain or deliberately chipping the blade. But if I did not value the knife, if no one valued the knife, nothing morally wrong would be done to the knife by ruining it because the knife itself has no independent moral standing.

Contrast the value of the knife to the value of my nephew. Both have intrinsic value$_1$ in that both are sources of ultimate value for me rather than means to some other valuable end. But unlike the knife, my nephew has intrinsic value$_2$. If I stop valuing him, indeed if no one were to value him, he does not lose moral considerability. He must figure in moral deliberations *for his own sake* whether I value him or not.

It is possible for a thing to possess intrinsic value$_1$ without being intrinsically valuable in this second sense (i.e., without having any intrinsic value$_2$), and the reverse is also true: a thing can be morally considerable without being a source of ultimate value, non-instrumental value. As Jamieson points out, there is no contradiction in believing that sentience bestows moral considerability while rejecting the belief that sentience—the capacity to experience pleasure and pain—is of ultimate value (Jamieson 2008, 70). To say that wilderness has intrinsic value$_2$ would be to say that wilderness itself is morally considerable *for its own sake* and not just because it is a source of instrumental or ultimate value to other morally considering beings.

Intrinsic Value as Non-Relational Value

Intrinsic value in a third sense ("intrinsic value$_3$") is sometimes called "inherent value" to designate a sense of non-relational value famously expounded by G. E. Moore. "To say that a kind of value is intrinsic," writes Moore, "means merely that the question whether a thing possess it, and in what degree it possesses it, depends solely on the intrinsic nature of the thing in question" (Moore 1922, 260). The idea here is that for a thing to have intrinsic value in this third sense, no appeal can be made to anything beyond it to explain the value. The value must be inherent in the properties of the thing in question and not depend on relations of any kind with any other thing.

John O'Neill draws attention to the fact that intrinsic value$_3$ may be of little use for environmental activists. "Many of the properties that are central to environmental valuation—rarity, species richness, biodiversity—are non-intrinsic in this Moorean sense" (O'Neill 2001, 167). Rarity, for example, is necessarily a relational property. So while rarity may have intrinsic value$_1$ inasmuch as the value need not be instrumental, that would not necessarily give it intrinsic value$_3$. To claim that wilderness has intrinsic value$_3$ would be to claim that wilderness is valuable for its inherent properties alone, and that we need not point to relations between wilderness and other things to understand its value.

Intrinsic Value as Value Independent of Valuers

Intrinsic value in a fourth and final sense ("intrinsic value$_4$") is value that exists independent of any valuer. For example, if you believe that the Chamonix Valley is valuable even if there exist no beings capable of valuing it, then you believe the Chamonix Valley has intrinsic value$_4$. Intrinsic value$_4$ is distinguished from intrinsic value$_3$ since an absence of valuers does not imply an absence of relations upon which the value depends.

Suppose that no one alive today values the Chamonix Valley. Further suppose that the valley itself is not a morally considerable being. It is still possible to ascribe value to the Chamonix Valley without reaching for intrinsic value$_4$. Even if no one now values the valley's combination of glaciers, trees, pinnacles, and cliffs, we can surely recognize that the valley is a potential source of value for other valuers. But intrinsic value$_4$ is not the value something has even when it is not actively being valued; is it the value it has even in the absence of *all possible valuation*, the value it has if no being ever does, or ever could, value it. To claim that wilderness is intrinsically valuable in this fourth sense would be to claim that, absent all possibility of valuation by a valuing being, wilderness remains a thing of value.[3]

ANTHROPOCENTRISM AND NONANTHROPOCENTRISM

Anthropocentrism, as a concept of value, assumes the moral superiority of humans over other beings. It further assumes that in all moral deliberations, all value should ultimately be reduced to the value for, or of, human beings. So while an anthropocentrist could recognize the value of a wetland for migrating birds, this value must always reduce to a human value, and it must always be trumped by a conflicting human-centered value (say, draining the wetland to plant crops). In anthropocentrism, human value and the value of humans are paramount. With a handful of exceptions (Bentham's utilitarianism being one), the history of Western moral philosophy has been anthropocentric, thus explaining Richard Routley's plea for a new, an environmental, ethic.[4] The concepts of anthropocentrism and nonanthropocentrism are connected to the intrinsic value debate inasmuch as they are concerned with moral considerability and the proper ascription of intrinsic value$_2$.

"When environmental ethics emerged as a new sub-discipline of philosophy in the early 1970s," write Brennan and Lo, "it did so by posing a challenge to traditional anthropocentrism" (Brennan and Lo 2015). Those who called for a new, an environmental ethic, realized that anthropocentrism potentially left the natural world morally vulnerable. If or when the good of humans and the good of the nonhuman natural world conflict, anthropocentrism has little to offer in defense of nature. At best, one can attempt to show that human interests and the interest of the natural world are one and the same. Such was the successful strategy of Rachel Carson in her book *Silent Spring* (Carson 1962) and of Al Gore in his documentary *An Inconvenient Truth*. When applicable, appeals to the convergence of human interest and natural interests remain environmentalism's most potent political motivator.

But human interests and the interests of the nonhuman natural world frequently come apart. Only the most intransigent environmentalist would refuse to acknowledge that certain kinds of farming, fishing, mining, human habitation, and mechanized transportation *are* of value to present and future human beings even while they do variable measures of harm to the natural world. Going green, so to speak, only sometimes optimizes the satisfaction of human interests, present or future.[5]

Realizing that human interests and the interests of the nonhuman natural world cannot always be aligned, and eager to safeguard the nonhuman natural world, early environmental ethicists sought to replace anthropocentric ethics with nonanthropocentric ethics. A nonanthropocentric ethics is any ethic that does not assume, *prima facie*, the moral superiority of humans over other beings, and does not believe that all moral deliberations should be reduced to deliberations about what is valuable for human beings. The idea is that if some form of nonanthropocentrism is true it will be of enormous use to those wishing to protect the nonhuman natural world, for even in the event that human interests run contrary to nonhuman natural interests, a nonanthropocentric ethic does not cede primacy to human beings as anthropocentrism must.

On its own, nonanthropocentrism merely signals the rejection of anthropocentrism. It leaves open the question as to what should replace *anthropos* as the center of our moral concern. Three varieties of nonanthropocentrism have prominence in environmental ethics: sentientism, biocentrism, and ecocentrism.

Sentientism

Sentientism is the position that all and only sentient beings are morally considerable, and all moral deliberations ought to take into consideration that which is of value to and for sentient beings. As we saw in chapter 2, sentientism is operative in the OFW. Here I will briefly review three versions of sentientism as developed by Peter Singer (1990), Tom Regan (1983), and Joel Feinberg (1974).

In *Animal Liberation* Singer argues that moral considerability requires that a subject have the capacity to experience pleasure and pain. For him, this capacity is a necessary and sufficient condition for moral considerability.[6] Following in the utilitarian moral tradition of Bentham and Mill, Singer writes: "The capacity for suffering and enjoyment is a prerequisite for having interests at all, a condition that must be satisfied before we can speak of interests in a meaningful way" (Singer 1990, 7). Lacking the capacity to experience pleasure or pain, a tree has no interest in not being kicked; a cat, however, does have an interest in not being kicked given that it would suffer as a result. Singer understands "the capacity to experience" as equivalent to "consciousness of."

Feinberg and Regan, though both sentientists, have argued that the capacity for pleasure and pain is not enough to establish moral standing. For Feinberg, having an interest entails more than just feeling pain or pleasure, because:

> an interest, however the concept is finally to be analyzed, presupposes at least rudimentary cognitive equipment. Interests are compounded somehow out of *desires* and *aims*—both of which presuppose something like beliefs, or cognitive awareness . . . mere brute longings unmediated by beliefs—longings for one knows not what—might be a primitive form of consciousness . . . but they are altogether different from the sort of thing we mean by "desire," especially when we speak of human beings. (Feinberg 1974, 52–53)

Unless a being is capable of consciously imagining and aiming at its future, it doesn't really have interests and thus cannot be considered morally considerable. The result for Feinberg is that only sentient beings are morally considerable, but not all sentient beings are morally considerable. The number of species included in Feinberg's set of morally considerable beings will be significantly smaller than Singer's.

In *The Case for Animal Rights*, Regan develops a version of sentientism to defend the rights of some animals. Like Feinberg, he does not think that the mere capacity to experience pleasure and pain is enough to grant moral standing. Rather, he argues that all and only beings that meet his "subject of a life" criterion deserve moral considerability (Regan 1983, 243). Being the subject of a life entails having feelings, memories, desires, and a sense of one's future; it requires that one cares about, or at least has the capacity to care about, one's own welfare. Regan's case for animal rights rests on the fact that humans are not the only animals who meet this criterion, though, as was the case with Feinberg, Regan's sentientism will deny an ascription of moral considerability to many more animals than Singer's.

Biocentrism

Biocentrism is the position that all and only living beings are morally considerable, and all moral deliberations ought to take into account that which is of value to and for living beings. In contrast to sentientism, biocentrism extends moral considerability to nonsentient organisms. Just as sentientists claim that anthropocentrists are privileging the morally arbitrary feature of belonging to the genus *homo*, biocentrists claim that sentientists are privileging the morally arbitrary feature of sentience. Thus Kenneth Goodpaster states that "nothing short of being alive seems to me to be a plausible and nonarbitrary criterion" for moral considerability (Goodpaster 1978, 310).

Goodpaster, Paul Taylor (2015), and Robin Attfield (1981,1987) have all advocated biocentric positions. Goodpaster argues that we are not justified in privileging sentience as the criterion for moral standing, as sentience is just a biological adaptation that allows certain kinds of organisms to respond to their needs. But why restrict the moral community based on the biological means by which an organism functions? In the evolutionary struggle for existence, some organisms have found sentience useful while other organisms have succeeded in virtue of different capacities and dispositions. For example, plants do not feel pain, but when threatened by hungry caterpillars some plants have a mechanism by which they alert their neighbors to the danger. The alerted plants increase their production of a chemical that makes their leaves tougher and less desirable to chew, thus discouraging the grazing caterpillars (Goudarzi 2007).

Goodpaster and Taylor also fault sentientism for supposing that the capacity for experiences (be it in Singer's, Regan's, or Feinberg's sense) is a necessary condition for having interests and thus being moral considerable. They point to the fact that each organism is "a teleological center of life, pursuing its own good in its own way" (Taylor 2015, 223) and conclude that every being with a good has an interest in having this good satisfied whether or not it is conscious of this good. On this interpretation, a plant has interests no less than a primate has interests. For example, it is in a plant's interest to have access to water, nutrients, and sunlight; it is in its interest that its roots remain embedded in the soil and that it is not devoured by pests. (There is at the very least some slippage in Taylor's account in this regard inasmuch as he recognizes a difference between saying that something *has an interest*—i.e., there is something good for it—and saying that it *is interested*—i.e., that it takes an interest in or wants that good.)[7] Attfield adds to the biocentric position by suggesting that plants, like humans, are capable of flourishing so long as their interests are satisfied (Attfield 1981, 1987).

Ecocentrism

Ecocentrism is a position that ascribes moral considerability to ecosystems. It claims that moral deliberations ought to consider what is of value to and for ecosystems.[8] The position emerged as our understanding of the science of ecology increased. If the good of individual organisms can only be understood in relation to the good of some environmental whole, some ecological system, then perhaps ecosystems are the proper object of environmental moral concern. Most ecocentrists do not, however, claim that all and only ecosystems are morally considerable given the repugnant implication that this would exclude human beings from moral considerability and make them valuable only as component parts of an ecosystem.

It is worth noting that most environmentalists are motivated to protect natural ecological systems in their totality rather than just individual organisms here and there. Environmentalists rightly worry that neither sentientism nor biocentrism can provide the philosophical justification they desire. As a result, if one's moral intuition reports that a forest has moral worth *qua* forest (rather than as a home for morally considerable beings), then one will have to look beyond sentientism and biocentrism to justify that intuition.

Ecocentrism is also a reaction to perceived difficulties in sentientism and biocentrism. The extension of moral considerability (whether based on considerations of welfare or of rights) might, as Jamieson wryly speculates, lead to a "lawyer's paradise in which every living thing has rights against every other living thing. Can a wildebeest sue a lion for violating his right to life? Do elephants have rights to take acacia trees or do acacia trees have rights to be protected?" (Jamieson 2008, 149). Rhetorical or not, such questions are troubling for any nonanthropocentric ethic seeking to widen the circle of moral considerability. If we focus on the good of the ecological community as a community, perhaps such questions lose their force.[9]

Aldo Leopold's land ethic was the first attempt to systemize the ecocentric position and it remains the paradigmatic example. "The land ethic," he writes, "simply enlarges the boundaries of the community to include soils, waters, plants, and animals, or collectively: the land." The land ethic "changes the role of Homo sapiens from conqueror of the land-community to plain member and citizen of it. It implies respect for his fellow members, and also respect for the community" (Leopold 2002, 28). Leopold speculates on the impossibility that "an ethical relation to the land can exist without love, respect, and admiration for land, and high regard for its value." He continues: "By value, I of course mean something far broader than mere economic value; *I mean value in the philosophical sense*" (ibid., 31 emphasis added).

Joseph DesJardins argues that a kind of ethical holism emerges from the land ethic. In this ethical holism, what is "Right and wrong is a function of the well-being of the community, not of its constituent members" (DesJardins 2006, 184). DesJardins further contends that it is a necessary implication of Leopold's land ethic that it is "the 'land community' that is granted moral standing." If Leopold is correct, "We now ought to grant moral standing to communities, symbolically represented as the land" (ibid., 181).

Leopold's ecocentrism leads him to propose the following maxim: "A thing is right when it tends to preserve the integrity, stability, and beauty of the biotic community. It is wrong when it tends otherwise" (Leopold 2002, 32). But how does he arrive at this normative conclusion? By accepting what he takes to be the natural facts of ecological science and inferring ethical values. Two ecological facts are of particular significance, as is one ecological supposition. The first fact, as mentioned, is that all life is interconnected: "Each species, including ourselves, is a link in many chains" (ibid., 29). The second is the fact that the land itself is integral to this chain as a source and conductor of life-giving energy:

> Land then, is not merely soil: it is a fountain of energy flowing through a circuit of soils and plants and animals. Food chains are living channels which conduct energy upwards; death and decay return it to the soil. The circuit is not closed; some energy is dissipated in decay, some is added by absorption from the air, some is stored in soils, peats, and long lived forests but it is a sustained circuit, like a slowly augmented revolving fund of life. (Ibid., 29)

Additionally, building upon what he takes to be ecological fact and borrowing ideas from the Russian mathematician and esoteric philosopher Pyotr

Ouspensky, Leopold considers that the earth itself might be alive, or at least should be thought of as being alive (see DesJardins 2006, 185). "Philosophy, then, suggests one reason why we cannot destroy the earth with moral impunity; namely that the 'dead' earth is an organism possessing a certain kind and degree of life, which we intuitively respect as such" (Leopold 1991, 95). If the ecosystems or the land or the earth is alive, then the arguments for biocentrism apply *mutatis mutandis*.

Holmes Rolston III has also sought to use the science of ecology to advance the case for ecocentrism. "The ecologist," he writes, "finds that ecosystems are objectively satisfactory communities in the sense that organismic needs are sufficiently met for species to survive and flourish." Moreover, "the critical ethicist finds . . . that ecosystems are satisfactory communities to which to attach duty. Our concern must be for the fundamental unit of survival" (Rolston 2002, 37). As was the case with Leopold, the argument is that since ecological communities generate and sustain life, and since living beings are morally considerable, the system that generates and sustains these beings must be morally considerable.

Rolston concedes that an ecosystem has no value for itself—it is not a valuing entity—but claims that it still can have value in itself. "Though [an ecosystem] is a value producer, it is not a value owner" (ibid., 37). Rolston further claims that the traditional intrinsic/instrumental binary is inadequate to capture the value of ecosystems. He proposes a third category: systemic value. In the case of systemic value, "Duties arise in encounters with the system that projects and protects these member components in the biotic community" (ibid., 38). He summarizes his ecocentric view in the following way:

> Those who have traveled partway into environmental ethics will say that ecosystems are of value because they contribute to animal experiences or to organismic life. But the really conservative [conservationist], radical view sees that the stability, integrity, and beauty of biotic communities are what are most fundamentally to be conserved. (Ibid.)

CRITIQUE OF INTRINSIC VALUE

This section will argue that intrinsic value$_3$ (value that is inherent and non-relational) and intrinsic value$_4$ (value in the absence of possible valuers) should have no bearing on the wilderness debate; hence, any argument on behalf of wilderness preservation that ascribes intrinsic value to wilderness can only do so because its value is an ultimate value or because its value is based upon considerations of moral considerability. In other words, any argument for the intrinsic value of the wilderness must make an appeal to the conception of intrinsic value$_1$ or intrinsic value$_2$. I see no reason to question whether wilderness can be of non-instrumental, ultimate value for some valuing being—it is for me and many people I know. The suggestion that wilderness is morally considerable is more complicated and will be treated later. I also take it that ascriptions of instrumental value to wilderness are uncontroversial, whatever one may believe about its intrinsic value.

Critique of Appeals to Intrinsic Value$_3$

One might try to argue for the intrinsic value of wilderness by supposing the third sense of intrinsic value discussed above. Intrinsic value$_3$ corresponds to the Moorean sense of intrinsic value as non-relational value. But, as we will see more fully in chapter 4, most arguments in defense of wilderness preservation cite values that are not intrinsic$_3$ to wilderness. For example, if one points, as many do, to the role that wilderness plays in providing raw resources for recreation and industry, or the way in which wilderness can act as a laboratory for evolution, or the possible abundance of miracle drugs waiting to be discovered therein, one cannot claim to be ascribing intrinsic value$_3$ to wilderness. It is the case that most of the arguments for the preservation of nature are based on values that cannot be considered non-relational and inherent in the properties of wilderness *qua* wilderness.

Of course, just because few actually make the argument that wilderness has intrinsic value$_3$ does not mean that such an argument cannot be made. But there are two other reasons to doubt that value in this sense can pertain to the value of wilderness. If wilderness has value *qua* wilderness—that is, if it has as untrammeled nature retaining its primeval character, insignificantly influenced by human activity or presence—then the value of wilderness is dependent on wilderness instantiating a relation of non-identity and noninterference with the human world. As will be shown in chapter 4, an entirely artificial world that nonetheless includes areas that are sensorially and functionally equivalent to wilderness areas would not be considered to have the same value as a world with wilderness precisely because the essential value of wilderness emerges as the value of the existence of a domain of natural world that is neither created nor controlled by human beings. Because we cannot understand such a valuation of wilderness *qua* wilderness without recourse to a relation between the human and nonhuman world, it is difficult to see how the value of wilderness could be said to obtain simply by virtue of its intrinsic properties

The second reason to doubt a reasonable ascription of intrinsic value$_3$ to wilderness is that arguments for it, like arguments for intrinsic value$_4$, must take the form of isolation tests. As we will see in "Critique of Appeals to Intrinsic Value$_4$", isolation tests may be the only means by which one may establish inherent value or value in the absence of valuers, but this fact does nothing to mitigate the inadequacy of the method for establishing wilderness as intrinsically valuable in the third or fourth senses of the term. So while we might admit the metaethical possibility of wilderness possessing intrinsic value$_3$, we would still face the epistemic difficulty of explaining how we came to know this.

Critique of Appeals to Intrinsic Value$_4$

One might also try to demonstrate the wilderness' intrinsic value by taking it in the sense of "intrinsic value$_4$," i.e., the concept of a value that is intrinsic by virtue of its alleged independence of any valuer. Intrinsic value in this sense has been something of a Holy Grail for environmental ethics: mysterious, long hoped for, and much sought after. Yet like the Grail, no one has found it and it is questionable whether there is anything to find.

Intrinsic value$_4$, like intrinsic value$_3$, is argued for with what Moore called isolation tests. Isolation tests ask one to consider some entity or state of affairs in isolation, absent all other morally significant variables, and then consider whether the entity or state of affairs would still be valuable (or good). Richard and Val Routley's now famous "last man" scenario is a kind of isolation test, and it aptly demonstrates the hope that environmental ethicists placed in the ideas of nonanthropocentrism and intrinsic value$_4$. Last man scenarios also demonstrate, I submit, the futility of appealing to intrinsic value$_4$, given the weakness of the arguments on its behalf. Here is the "last man" scenario in the Routleys' own words:

> The last man (or person) surviving the collapse of the world system lays about him, eliminating, as far as he can, every living thing, animal or plant (but painlessly if you like, as at the best abattoirs). What he does is quite permissible according to basic chauvinism, but on environmental grounds it is wrong. Moreover one does not have to be committed to esoteric values to regard Mr. Last Man as behaving badly and destroying things of value. (Routley and Routley 1980, 124)

According to anthropocentrism, or basic chauvinism, the last man does nothing wrong and destroys nothing of value.[10] But the Routleys find it intuitively obvious, morally self-evident, that the last man does do something wrong and does destroys something of value. On their view, then, anthropocentrism is mistaken and human beings cannot be the loci of all moral value.

There is much left wanting in the Routleys' presentation of the last man scenario as a demonstration of intrinsic value$_4$ (or any other kind of intrinsic value).[11] If the Routleys' chief aim is to discredit anthropocentrism, the scenario may elicit a useful intuition inasmuch as it acknowledges the presence of animals; if even one of these animals is sentient, then there is at least one morally considerable being suffering harm. So the intuition that the last man does something wrong could be easily explained by the fact that the last man harms sentient beings, and by endorsing some version of sentientism we can makes sense of the wrongness. Given what we know of evolution, one could also claim that the last man acts wrongly by depriving any future, yet to evolve, sentient and valuing beings of the chance to value anything. And even if we stipulate that there will be no such evolution, biocentrists could argue that the nonsentient plant and animal life destroyed by the last man possess the value (intrinsic value$_2$) of being morally considerable beings. In sum, the Routleys' last man scenario leaves open the possibility that other beings endowed with intrinsic value$_2$ still exist, and the possibility that other beings capable of valuing might exist in the future. No recourse to intrinsic value$_4$ is needed to explain why the Routleys' last man does something wrong.

It seems, moreover, that the last man acts wrongly on purely anthropocentric grounds. A person who spends his last moments on earth engaged in the wonton destruction of life and beauty exhibits what most regard as a contemptible character; he is a repugnant human being. Significant work has been done on environmental virtue ethics to explain exactly why, from an anthropocentric point of view, there is something morally deficient about environmental degradation, especially the kind imagined in the last man scenario.[12] It is possible, however, to augment the last man scenario such that it constitutes an isolation test possible of establishing the wilderness' intrinsic value$_4$.[13]

Consider the following revised version that I will call the "last human" scenario. The last surviving human has only a few hours left to live. There will be no more humans after her. All other life is already dead, and there will be no more life in the future. Before expiring, the last human sets off a series of explosions that destroys the earth's geology. The Grand Canyon, Iguazu Falls, Ayer's Rock, Annapurna and so on are reduced to rubble. Then she dies.

All last man scenarios are meant to elicit the intuition that the individual acted wrongly and destroyed something of value. Further, they are often meant to show that our moral intuitions about the wrongness of the act are justified only if we acknowledge the existence of intrinsic value in the fourth sense discussed above. That is to say, given our belief that the last man acted wrongly and destroyed something of value, we are supposed to acknowledge the existence of intrinsic value$_4$, value in the absence of a possible valuer. But does the last human (which is considerably stronger than the Routleys' last man scenario) lead to a cogent argument for the existence of something akin to wilderness' intrinsic value$_4$?

If the question is "Did the last human act wrongly?," the virtue-based explanation is sufficient to show that she did, and the act remains wrong whether or not something can have value in the absence of a valuer. But if the question is "Did the last human destroy something of value?" a more nuanced answer is required.

The last human eliminates the possibility of appealing to the moral considerability of sentient or nonsentient life—both are already gone. And it eliminates the possibility that, at some point in the future, there will exist valuing creatures—there will be no more. So an argument for intrinsic value$_4$ from the last human scenario would go as follows:

P1—The last man did not deprive present or future valuing beings of anything of value.

P2—Yet the last man still destroyed something of value.

Conclusion—Therefore, something of value exists absent possible valuers.

To the best of my knowledge, responses to last man scenarios have never been collected, analyzed, and reported in anything other than an anecdotal way.[14] But let us assume (as the Routleys assumed for the purposes of their isolation test) that most people would agree, given a proper understanding the scenario, that the last human destroys something of value. Even then it is not necessary to postulate the existence of value in absence of valuers. There is a better explanation for our negative intuition.

Jamieson reminds us that even if a last man scenario stipulates the absence of all present and future valuers, some valuers are still part of the equation: specifically, *we* are.

> For we who are contemplating the world without valuers are ourselves valuers, and indeed we are contemplating the loss of that we find very valuable. Even if it is stipulated that we will never experience this world in either its preserved or destroyed state, we are already experiencing these states in our imagination, and it seems plausible that this is what governs our response to this thought-experiment. (Jamieson 2008, 74)

Jamieson is proposing a sort of error theory that would explain, without recourse to intrinsic value$_4$, why we are inclined to react as if the last man destroyed something of value. It is psychologically difficult to be a valuer here and now, contemplating the destruction of something we value, and not feel that something of value would be lost even if we can no longer value it. This psychological difficulty is what leads to the "error" of supposing that the only way to explain our lingering intuition that the last man destroys something of value is to postulate value in the absence of valuers.

I concur with Jamieson's analysis, and would add to it by saying that it is very difficult to stop ourselves from thinking of the earth as a *potential* source of value for some valuing creature. Even when we stipulate valuers out of existence, there is an impulse to think: "Yes, but what if there *was* one?" It is true that the earth remains a potential source of value in the absence of valuers. But admitting that something can remain a potential source of value in the absence of valuers does not establish intrinsic value$_4$ any more than acknowledging that an apple is a potential source for the perceptual experience of redness proves the experience of redness absent a certain kind of perceiving subject.

CRITIQUE OF NONANTHROPOCENTRISM

This section will expose flaws in biocentrism and ecocentrism, thereby arguing that sentientism is the only viable form of nonanthropocentrism, the significance of which is that an ascription of moral considerability to wilderness *qua* wilderness loses plausibility unless one is prepared to make the very strange argument that wilderness is sentient (more on this in chapter 4). As previously noted, debates about anthropocentrism and various forms of nonanthropocentrism are essentially debates about intrinsic value$_2$. I contend that nothing short of the capacity for experiences qualifies a being as morally considerable. To be sure, beings (living or not) that lack independent moral considerability frequently still have a role to play in our moral deliberations. But recognizing that trees and mountains should figure into our moral deliberations is very different than saying that the trees and mountains have moral standing.

As I will explain later in this chapter, while I ultimately find biocentrism and ecocentrism unviable, should my analysis prove to be mistaken—should it prove to be the case that either biocentrism or ecocentrism is correct—it would neither establish the moral considerability of wilderness *qua* wilderness nor lend itself to an argument in defense of wilderness *qua* wilderness. If anything, the moral considerability of all organisms or all ecosystems, or both, would add a new dimension to the OFW and provide yet another reason to potentially intervene on behalf of morally considerable entities.

Critique of Biocentrism

Biocentrism maintains that all living beings have independent moral standing, are morally considerable in their own right. Goodpaster argues that sentientism arbitrarily privileges a biological adaptation that enables experiences of pain and pleasure while dismissing as morally irrelevant different but equally complex biological adaptations in nonsentient creatures. Taylor and Goodpaster seem to be arguing that nonsentient organisms do have interests, when interests are understood as conditions that must be satisfied in order for an entity to achieve its teleological good, while Attfield adds that a creature with a teleological good is capable of flourishing. Assuming that it is good for a being to have its interests satisfied, then any being with interests is capable of being harmed to the extent that the satisfaction of its interests is thwarted.

In this context, "interest" stands for whatever allows that being to be what it is and do what it does, thereby flourishing as the kind of being it is; hence, trees have interests no less than people. It is in a tree's interest to have water and sunlight, not to be chopped down, and to avoid disease. Similarly, it is in an oyster's interest not to be shucked, squirted with lemon, and swallowed.

In support of the idea that a being can have interests without being sentient, Gary Varner argues that many human interests are similar to the interests of nonsentient organisms inasmuch as human sentience is irrelevant to the human need to satisfy these interests. For example, it is in our interest to absorb vitamin C, but this interest has nothing to do with our perception of the absorption or consciousness that it is even taking place (Varner 1998, chapter 3). The argument here is that if human interests, which are morally considerable, do not all depend on sentience, why should we restrict moral considerability to organisms with interests but without consciousness of these interests?

My primary objection to biocentrism is that, based on its own arguments, it would extend the domain of morally considerable beings far beyond just living beings. The resulting set of morally considerable beings becomes farcical. Biocentrists who set out to promote the moral considerability of organisms would be committed to promoting the moral considerability of anything that can be said to have a teleological function or a good of its own. Biocentrism would become *interestism*, a position I cannot see biocentrists endorsing. The following examples illustrate the potentially absurd implications of the biocentric position.

Artifacts, no less than living beings, have goods of their own that can be furthered or thwarted, and if the biocentrist account is maintained, they also have some sort of interests. For my bicycle to be a good bicycle it must have two wheels, both inflated to the proper pressure; it must have a well-oiled chain, responsive brakes, front and rear reflectors, a level surface on which to move and, ultimately, a rider. It is in the interest of my bicycle, *qua* bicycle, to have these features and conditions. If the interests go unsatisfied, the bicycle cannot do what it is meant to do, or at least not do it optimally. So it seems that the biocentric arguments ought to include my bicycle in the set of morally considerable beings.

Before turning to the biocentric response, consider the possibility that in using a teleological conception of the good to establish that nonsentient beings can have goods of their own and interests, Goodpaster, Taylor, and Attfield might actually be making a stronger case for the moral considerability of my bicycle than for a tree. Taylor tells us that even a nonsentient organism is "a teleological center of life, pursuing its own good in its own way" (Taylor 2015, 223). But is it? What is the function of a tree, the final cause? Teleology requires a purpose, a function. I submit that my bicycle can be understood teleologically far easier, and far more coherently, than a tree. The biocentrists could at this point revert to some form of Aristotelianism, but it would be suspect for an ethical position grounded in the modern science of biology to suddenly reach back to an Aristotelian conception of life when doing so proves ethically convenient. The idea that organisms, sentient or otherwise, have an absolute *telos* with ethical significance is an idea that must be rejected. Bernard Williams reminds us "The first and hardest lesson of Darwinism, that there is no such teleology at all, and that there is no orchestral score provided from anywhere according to which human beings have a special part to play, still has to find its way into ethical thought" (Williams 1985: 110). If Darwinism—which biocentrists accept when discussing biology—causes us to relinquish the hope of an absolute biological human *telos* performing an ethical function, we must also relinquish the hope that such a *telos* exists for other organisms. In the end, it is possible that teleological conception of the good leading to interests has a better chance of establishing moral considerably for bicycles than it does for trees.

Suppose, though, that the poverty of a teleological basis for interests does not trouble all biocentrists. Biocentrists might respond that trees and bicycles are importantly different in that a tree, unlike my bicycle, *pursues* its own interests by responding to stimuli: the branches reach for sunlight, the roots search for water, bark regenerates to provide protection. Even if it is in the interest of my bicycle to have inflated tires, the bicycle does not pursue this interest.

But consider the example of my computer. It is in the interest of my computer to have a power source and a charged battery, to have an ample supply of memory, and to steer clear of viruses and eliminate them if infected. The computer itself takes measures to satisfy these interests. When the battery is low it shifts to an emergency power-saving regime; when low on memory it refuses certain downloads and prompts me to make space or add space; and to defend against viruses the computer initiates and operates regular scans, taking aggressive countermeasures if one is detected. If having interests simply means having a teleological orientation toward some good such that the satisfaction of interests furthers this good, and if all it takes for an individual being to be morally considerable is that it has such a good and is capable of pursuing its good, then computers (and many other human artifacts) would be as morally considerable as trees and oysters.

Now the biocentrists might now respond that computers, unlike trees, are anthropogenic. The computer only has interests because we made it, and we made it such that it has interests. Trees, however, were not created by humans, and have interests independent of human beings. Apart from the fact that I find it easier to establish teleology for artifacts than for organisms, it is not clear, morally, why a being's anthropogenic origin (or lack thereof) should matter. If a being has interests, as biocentrists understand interests, it has them regardless of where or how it acquired them. It is surely arbitrary to insert the proviso "that are not of human origin" into the biocentric argument. Moreover, as Jamieson argues, if anthropogenic interests do not deserve moral consideration, then the interests of even sentient human organisms born through in-vitro fertilization, cloning, or with some kind of genetic manipulation must lose moral standing as well (Jamieson 2008, 148).

An appeal to interests, as they are construed by biocentrists, as the criterion of moral considerability would unacceptably and comically broaden the moral community to include all manner of machines, and the "smarter" machines get, the more actively they will attempt to promote their interests. And it will not do to claim suddenly that only the interests of organic, non-anthropogenic beings are of moral concern. Such a move would be no less arbitrary than the anthropocentrist trying to claim that even though animals suffer, only human suffering matters.

What about the biocentric claim that sentientism also privileges a morally arbitrary feature, i.e., sentience? As we saw, such a belief led Goodpaster to assert: "nothing short of *being alive* seems to me to be a plausible and nonarbitrary criterion" (Goodpaster 1978, 310). But is sentience morally arbitrary? I do not think that is. To the contrary, I believe that sentientists are on firm ground in using sentience to ascribe moral considerability. On this point Jamieson writes:

> For the sentientist, the reason a person has interests and a car [or some other artifact] does not is that what happens to the person matters to her, while nothing matters to the car. In this respect, the car and the tree are similar and the person is different: it matters to the person that her interests are respected, but not to the tree or to the car. We may prefer that the car or the tree be in tiptop condition, but that is our preference, not theirs. (Jamieson 2008, 147)

It is because sentient beings care what happens to themselves and their interests, and because nonsentient beings do not, that sentience is not an arbitrary criterion for moral considerability. "What is essential for having interests," continues Jamieson, "is that it matters to the being what happens to her. This is what is true of humans and many other animals, and what is not true of plants" (ibid., 148). Bernard Williams makes the same point in a slightly different way when he argues that we should only care about the interests of beings that can have experiences (Williams 1994, 47–48). Sentient beings can have experiences. Plants and computers cannot (for the time being).

The moral relevance of sentience, the reason it is not a morally arbitrary feature, is that sentience is a necessary condition for experiences and experiences are a necessary condition for a conception of interests that does not expand the moral community to include cars, bicycles, and computers (employing a minimal conception of experience that entails consciousness of one's suffering and satisfaction). Moreover, sentience allows for an understanding of interests that does not rely on a pre-Darwinian conception of teleology in nature, a conception that biocentrists reject when they do science, but want to invoke when they do ethics.[15]

To care about one's own interests, to be capable of experiences, is, to use Regan's term, to be the subject of a life rather than merely to be alive. Now, some might claim that plants or indeed computers have experiences and care about what happens to them. But notice that should it prove to be the case that plants or computers have experiences and care about what happens to them such that they should be considered subjects of a life, it still would not support the biocentric position. Rather, it would merely widen the set of beings already given moral standing by sentientism.[16]

Before moving on to consider ecocentrism, it is worth noting that some biologists have sought to replace teleology and its cumbersome Aristotelian baggage with what they call teleonomy (Pittendrigh 1958, Mayr 1965, Williams 1966). Could teleonomy make the biocentric case where teleology comes up short?

I do not think that it can. Teleonomy is the quality of apparent purposefulness of structure or function in living organisms due to evolutionary adaptation. Teleonomy recognizes goal-directed activity within organisms, and it recognizes that to ignore this activity would lead to impoverished analysis; yet unlike teleology it remains silent on final causes. As biologist Ernst Mayr puts it, a teleonomic system is one "operating on the basis of a program of coded information" (Mayr 1965, 42). The rise of teleonomic analysis in biology led David Hull to report the following memorable simile:

> Haldane [a prominent biologist in first half of the twentieth century] can be found remarking, "Teleology is like a mistress to a biologist: he cannot live without her but he's unwilling to be seen with her in public." Today the mistress has become a lawfully wedded wife. Biologists no longer feel obligated to apologize for

their use of teleological language; they flaunt it. The only concession which they make to its disreputable past is to rename it "teleonomy." (Hull 1982)

I will not attempt to evaluate the legitimacy of teleonomy as a biological concept, and I want to make it clear that I am not disputing the quality of apparent purposefulness of structure and function in living organisms due to evolutionary adaptation. Nor am I suggesting that this apparent purposefulness lacks moral relevance. Indeed, I think Philippa Foot and Rosalind Hursthouse have convincingly argued that an understanding of an organism's apparent purposiveness is important in establishing what it means for that organism to flourish (Hursthouse 1999, Foot 2001).[17] What I dispute is that teleonomy, which gives up on final causes, is sufficient to establish moral considerability (intrinsic value$_2$) for living beings. An adoption of teleonomy will not help the biocentrist. Even if biocentrists switch from talk of teleology to talk of teleonomy, the biocentric claim—which is fundamentally moral rather biological—is not strengthened.

Critique of Ecocentrism

Ecocentrism is the position that ecosystems, rather than individual organisms, should be the loci of value on which environmental ethics is based, and that ecosystems are moral considerable. In "Anthropocentrism and Nonanthropocentrism" I explained that one motivation for ecocentrism was to avoid the practical problems associated with biocentrism (recall Jamieson asking, *inter alia*, whether wildebeests have the right to sue lions for harm and loss of life). But even supposing ecocentrism avoids the practical difficulties associated with biocentrism, it suffers its own complications.[18]

First, the practical problems associated with ecocentrism are at least equal to those of biocentrism. I already noted that ecosystems are vague in that it is hard, if not impossible, to identify where one begins and ends. They also overlap, and one ecosystem might be entirely enclosed within another ecosystem. The vagueness isn't an overwhelming concern for the science of ecology (any more than the vagueness of baldness is of overwhelming concern for the makers of Propecia) but it is of critical ethical concern. If ecosystems are meant to be the primary object of concern in environmental ethics, and if they deserve moral consideration as Leopold, Rolston, and others think they do, we must at least be able to identity what, when, and where they are (see Jamieson 2008, 150–51).

A second concern is whether it really makes sense to conceive of ecosystems as independent entities in anything other than a metaphorical way. Jamieson suggests that ecosystems are like constellations: the individual stars exist, but the constellation is a projection. It may be useful for ecologists to speak about ecosystems, but that does not give them existence as independent entities (ibid., 151).

DesJardins argues that an ecocentrist like Leopold is using an organic model of ecology that seeks to understand ecosystems as organisms, or at least functionally equivalent to organisms. In the organic model, the biota compromising an ecosystem stand in relation to the ecosystem the way individual organs stand in relation to a body. But since the work of Arthur Tansley the organic model is no longer credible. "Tansley argued," writes DesJardins, "that ecosystems can be viewed as organisms only in a metaphorical way."

> They are not literally organisms because individuals within an ecosystem, unlike the individual organs of a body, could exist outside the organism. Ecosystems do not have "unity and definiteness" of real organisms, and their constituent parts are quite capable of moving into other systems and becoming full members of them. This independence means that members of an ecosystem are quite unlike the organs of body. (DesJardins 2006, 193)

The idea that the earth itself is a living being is an empirical hypothesis lacking empirical evidence. Moreover, while the belief that ecosystems are organisms can be conceptually useful, that utility provides no warrant for presuming that such concepts correspond to actual things in the world.

A third concern is that ecocentrism, as Regan puts it, "might be fairly dubbed 'environmental fascism'" (Regan 1983, 362). Interestingly, the objection is a corollary to the practical objection against overly extending the moral community that ecocentrists sometimes make against biocentrists. In suggesting that ecocentrism is fascist, Regan is objecting to the way the good or right of every individual becomes subservient to the good or right of the ecosystem. In a fascist state, the welfare of each citizen (to the extent that their welfare matters at all) is always second to the welfare of the state; the good of the individual is subservient to the good of the whole, and it is subservient not for the sake of better serving the good of the individual. The good of the whole is the ultimate moral concern. In an ecocentric moral system, the welfare of any individual plant or animal (and potentially any human being) is secondary to the welfare of the ecosystem. "The implications of this view," writes Regan, "include the clear prospect that the individual may be sacrificed for the greater biotic good, in the name of 'integrity, stability, and beauty of the biotic community.' It is difficult to see how the notion of the rights of the individual could find a home." (ibid., 361–62). If biocentrism is worrying because of the ceaseless proliferation of individual rights, ecocentrism is terrifying because it eliminates them.

Fourth, ecocentrism runs into Darwinian trouble no less than biocentrism. To suppose that there is some fixed integrity and stability to nature, some proper progression that morally ought to continue, is to project purpose and *telos* where none exists. DesJardins explains:

> When we speak of how predators "function" within an ecosystem, it is easy to think that wolves exist in order to prey on elk and other species and thus to maintain a natural stability and equilibrium. But the Darwinian explanation suggests that wolves prey on elk and other species simply because in the past this behavior proved adaptive and wolves that have done it have survived to reproduce. (DesJardins 2006, 188)

Again, if one is willing to commit to an Aristotelian view of nature, ecocentrism might have legs, though one would then need to reckon with Aristotle's moral prioritization of human beings. One will also have to explain why it makes sense to promote the stability of systems that naturally are unstable. DesJardin correctly asserts: "There may well not be a single ecosystem that develops through time."

> For example, over time the populations of a field might go through a series of ecological transformations from weeds to perennials and grasses, to shrubs, to pine forests, to oak forests. What would the "integrity and stability" of this system be? Should we seek to preserve the field as a home to prairie grasses and shrubs, preserve the locale once it reaches the stage of pine forest, or stay out altogether and let whatever happens happen? (Ibid., 186)

Fifth, even if one can see a way past all the other objections, one must be wary of becoming entangled in an is-ought problem (i.e., the problem of explaining how one moves from claims about natural facts to ethical prescriptions) as well an appeal to nature (i.e., the fallacious argument that because a thing is natural that thing is also and necessarily good). So much has been said on the is-ought problem that it would be unhelpful to attempt a cursory analysis here. I only note that ecocentrists must acknowledge that, even if their understanding of ecology is correct, even if nature does tend toward stability, integrity and beauty (often at the expense of individual rights and welfare), this fact does not entail the conclusion that nature, or humans acting as nature's proxy, *ought* to promote the stability, integrity, and beauty of the biotic community as a focus of our moral concern. In regard to an appeal to nature, the Stoics long ago advised *naturam sequi*—follow nature. But, as J. S. Mill sufficiently demonstrates, to follow nature would be to frequently follow the example of an amoral, indifferent, purposeless being that is entirely insensitive to the pain, hardship and sorrow wrought by its works. Perhaps in some things, for some reasons, it makes sense to follow nature. But as a moral maxim such advice is bankrupt (Mill 2000, 223–35).[19]

Finally, the strongest reason to reject ecocentrism is the same as the reason to reject biocentrism: ecosystems are not beings that care or can care what happens to them; they cannot have experiences and they are not subjects of a life. Williams suggests that "The idea of ascribing interests to species, natural phenomena and so on, as a way of making sense of our concern for these things, is part of a project of trying to extend into nature our concerns for each other, by moralizing our relations with nature" (Williams 1994, 49). If Williams is correct, then it is unsurprising that a figure like Leopold who advocates "love, respect, and admiration for land, and high regard for its value" would be inclined to propose an ethical system making it a moral duty to do just that (Leopold 2002, 31).

Echoing Williams, Jana Thompson asks: "why should it be bad for the plant's sake to live a short time rather than a longer time? One reason we find it so natural to suppose that it is better for an organism's sake that it be healthy and have a long, productive life is because this is what we want for ourselves and what we want for the plants we grow. Nevertheless, plants don't want anything" (Thompson 1990, 155).[20] The critique of biocentrism based on interests and experiences applies, *mutatis mutandis*, to ecocentrism.

Thompson furthers the critique of ecocentrism by arguing that if by simply having a good of their own ecological systems deserve moral standing, we open the door to giving moral considerability to other systems which, on no one's account, deserve it. "Virtually anything . . . can be regarded as a system . . . the relationship between several animals and plants, an ecological system, the planet Earth, a heart or a kidney, a molecule, an interacting system of molecules" (ibid., 156). Later she considers the fact that social systems, no less than ecological systems, have a good of their own (ibid., 157). Yet to ascribe independent moral standing to social systems such as governments, rather than seeing them as a useful conglomeration of individuals with moral standing, is to make the case for Regan's charge of environmental fascism.

Thompson concludes her refutation of ecocentrism with a question. If ecocentrism is:

> nonviable, if we are stuck with a sentient-being-centered ethic, then what about the needs of the environment? What do we say about the intuitions and attitudes of those people who think that we ought to preserve the wilderness, species, and nonsentient organisms even when these things have no instrumental value for human beings or any other sentient creatures? (Ibid., 160)

I believe questions like this, and the fear that they are unanswerable, motivates much environmental nonanthropocentrism. She then makes a provocative suggestion, proposing an argument "that something is valuable and therefore ought to be preserved because our lives and our conception of ourselves will be enhanced—in a spiritual sense—if we learn to appreciate it for what it is and we learn how to live with it in harmony" (ibid., 160). I will return to her suggestion in chapter 5.

CONCLUSION

I have provided reasons for thinking that sentientism is the only viable form of nonanthropocentrism. I remain neutral on the matter of which version of sentientism is ultimately correct. I also acknowledge that many biocentrists and ecocentrists will remain unconvinced. But while I think that establishing the unviability of biocentrism and ecocentrism would make it easier to dismiss appeals for the moral considerability (intrinsic value$_2$) of wilderness *qua* wilderness *a fortiori*, it is crucial to see that establishing the moral considerability of all organisms (biocentrism) or the moral considerability of ecosystems (ecocentrism) would not in itself lead to an argument in defense of wilderness.

If anything, establishing the moral considerability of all organisms and all ecosystems would lend itself to an altered version of the OFW. The only difference would be that, where the OFW only focused on the *pro tanto* reason we have for intervening in wilderness to protect or promote the welfare of sentient beings, the altered version would show that we have *pro tanto* reasons to intervene in wilderness to protect or promote the welfare (or interests or teleological good or flourishing or stability, integrity, and beauty) of all organisms and all ecosystems. Just as was the case with the OFW, this new argument from welfare would be qualified such that we only interfered if we were overwhelmingly likely to do more good than harm.

Furthermore, even if we were to acknowledge the moral considerability of all organisms and all ecosystems, this does not get us to the moral considerability of *wilderness*. I confess to being nonplussed when I try to think what it would mean for wilderness, which is a condition of the natural world, to have moral considerability. This is not to say that wilderness cannot and does not have *value*. It can and it does. The question is how and what kind. The point I wish to drive home is that anyone who finds my support for sentientism and my dismissal of biocentrism and ecocentrism unsatisfactory need not dismiss the subsequent arguments and conclusion concerning the value of wilderness. Perhaps I'm wrong about ecocentrism, but if I am, that doesn't mean I am wrong about wilderness.

It bears emphasizing that to reject biocentric and ecocentric appeals for the moral standing of organisms and ecosystems is not to in any way deny that organisms and ecosystems and the environment have a substantial role to play in our ethical lives and ethical deliberation. I agree with Taylor that a moral human being should adopt an ethic of respect for nature—I simply deny that this respect entails, warrants, or presupposes ascribing moral considerability to nonsentient life. I agree with Leopold that we should strive to love, respect, and admire the land. But I do not see why or how this agreement necessitates or allows ascribing moral standing to ecosystems. Finally, I agree with Rolston that ecosystems are "value producers without being value owners"; I further agree that we may well have duties toward these systems and the biota of which they are made. Still, none of this provides a reason to ascribe moral considerability to them. Rolston wants to introduce the term "systemic value." I am happy to accept the term, and to accept that systems have a certain kind of value, so long as the value is not supposed to be intrinsic value$_2$. For the purpose of avoiding unnecessary quarrels, we can accept that it is possible to have respect for, and to have duties that arise in relation to, entities that are not themselves morally considerable.

This chapter has argued that only two senses of intrinsic value—intrinsic value$_1$ and intrinsic value$_2$—could possibly apply to the wilderness. Given the arguments against ascribing intrinsic value$_2$ to nonsentient organisms and ecological systems, it appears indefensible to ascribe intrinsic value$_2$, i.e., the intrinsic value of moral considerability, to a condition of the natural world that is untrammeled, retaining its primeval character, insignificantly influenced by human activity, and so on. Sentience is required for intrinsic value$_2$, and wilderness is not sentient. (Though I repeat: even if biocentrism or ecocentrism prove to be correct, neither does anything to establish the moral considerability of *wilderness*).

In the next chapter, I will advance the claim that if wilderness has value, it can only be instrumental value and intrinsic value$_1$ by reviewing the Gaia hypothesis argument, an argument I take to be a last-ditch effort to establish wilderness as a morally considerable being. I will also review the arguments on behalf of wilderness preservation with an eye toward understanding the kind of value ascription on which they are based, and thus whether they are viable as responses to the OFW. I will then be in position to say what I take the value of wilderness *qua* wilderness to be and begin considering what kind of argument for wilderness is possible based purely on the value of wilderness *qua* wilderness.

NOTES

1. There are exceptions, notably Bryan Norton. In "Environmental Ethics and Weak Anthropocentrism" he argues that anthropocentrism is not the problem, only what he labels "strong" anthropocentrism. On the one hand, strong anthropocentrism is based on what he calls felt preferences: "any desire or need of a human individual that can at

least temporarily be sated by some specifiable experience of that individual." On the other hand, weak anthropocentrism is based on a felt preference that would only be desired after "careful deliberation" (Norton 1984: 134). Norton is essentially arguing that humans in idealized epistemic states would realize that the anthropocentric value of a sustainable, virtuous, compassionate, and just use of nature exceeds the value of gratifying immediate desires and needs. He claims that his mitigation of anthropocentrism is not analogous to Mill's mitigation of hedonism by introducing higher and lower pleasures (and then supposing all competent judges will choose the higher). I fail to see how the two are accounts are significantly different.

2. O'Neill (2001) and Jamieson (2008) provide the most comprehensive review of intrinsic value as it pertains to environmental ethics. This section is indebted to the work of both authors.

3. Anyone committed to intrinsic value$_4$ is necessarily committed to a realist metaethic. It is thus unsurprising, as Jamieson argues, that "Since the birth of environmental ethics, there has been a strong tendency to embrace realism" (Jamieson 2008, 48–49). The reason for this is that intrinsic value$_4$ requires moral realism, and if environmental ethics could prove (a) the existence of value absent valuers, and (b) that certain features of the natural world possess this value, it would have a powerful moral reason to protect such features from destruction regardless of human valuation.

4. One might point out that for much of history the good of humanity was thought to be subservient to the good (or well-being, or glory) of God, in which case much Western moral philosophy has been theocentric, not anthropocentric. This is a provocative line of thought, but most theocentric ethics still aim to advance the good of man. Even if the reason to be godly is ultimately God, it is still conceived of as fundamentally good *for* human beings to be pious, either because piety leads to a theological conception of *eudaimonia*, or because an otherworldly system of reward and punishment awaits each individual. I would argue that most theocentric ethical systems are still anthropocentric inasmuch as they express concern for, and offer guidance toward, that which is believed to be best for human beings, or at least for humanity. The question of whether an omnibenevolent God could ever command that which is *ultimately* inimical to the good of a human being is one I leave for the theologians. Thank you to Stacey Rice and Stephen Bunn for raising this issue in conversation.

5. One can still argue that going green is always the morally correct thing to do, though note that this commits one to some form of nonanthropocentrism.

6. Note that the OFW only claims that capacity to experience pleasure and pain is a sufficient condition for moral considerability.

7. Taylor is ambiguous on the question of whether plants have interests. He states that plants have a good of their own, and then immediately adds that having a good of one's own "does not entail that the being must have interests or take an interest in what affects its life for better or for worse," suggesting he thinks plants do not have interests, only some teleological good. But in the next breath he says: "We can act in a being's interest or contrary to its interests without its being interested in what we are doing in the sense of wanting or not wanting us do it." He then adds: "Yet it is undoubtedly the case that trees can be harmed or benefited by our actions." (Taylor 2015, 321). It is most charitable, I think, to assume that Taylor believes nonsentient

organisms have interests only in the sense that that they have goods of their own, the satisfaction of which would be in their interests whether or not they can experience the satisfaction.

8. Biologists know that the term 'ecosystem' is shot through with vagueness. Where do ecosystems begin? Where do they end? How should we understand ecosystems that are themselves constituent parts of other ecosystems? Here I follow Jamieson in understanding ecosystem to mean "an assemblage of organisms together with its environment" (Jamieson 2008, 151).

9. For an example of how biocentric moral extensionism can reach absurdity, see Cockell's earnest plea for the rights of microbes (Cockell 2004).

10. For the Routleys, basic chauvinism is the rough equivalent of liberal anthropocentrism. Explaining chauvinism, they write: "The liberal philosophy of the Western world holds that one should be able to do what he wishes, providing (1) that he does not harm others and (2) that he is not likely to harm himself irreparably" (Routley and Routley 1980, 117).

11. In fairness to the Routleys, the last man scenario was a rhetorically effective strategy of argumentation and an illuminating way to help others think about environmental ethics. It is to their credit that the scenario is still being discussed. I do not mean to fault them for failing to provide a knock-down proof for intrinsic value$_4$.

12. For a variety of virtue-based arguments that could explain why the last man acts wrongly without abandoning anthropocentrism or invoking intrinsic value$_4$ see Sandler 2007, Cafaro and Sandler 2005, and Hill 1983. Environmental virtue ethics faces its own criticism for attempting to ground environmental ethics in an account of human flourishing. It seems like an ethics grounded in human flourishing may be inescapably anthropocentric. For some, an anthropocentric environmental ethic is not only unpalatable but unacceptable. Critics of the virtue approach would charge that if the only reason to behave ethically toward the environment is to promote our own well-being (however that is ultimately constituted) we are still very far from have an *environmental* ethic, i.e., an ethic that aims at a good not grounded in the good of and for human beings.

13. Benson follows a similar strategy for his own purposes, though my augmentation of the scenario differs from his augmentations (Benson 2000, 18–25).

14. It would be a revealing piece of social scientific research to see how the responses break down by age, gender, class, nationality, etc.

15. I understand the impulse. I often feel that I would rather live in an Aristotelian universe, but my annoyance that Newton and Darwin have made a certain view of nature and ethics less tenable is poor justification for applying the implications of their theories *à la carte*.

16. At this juncture a biocentrist may introduce the problem of marginal cases. It is unclear whether all human beings, simply by virtue of being human beings, care what happens to them, have experiences, or can be considered subjects of a life. Those who cannot are sometimes called marginal cases. Examples include very young infants, the severely mentally disabled, individuals with late-stage Alzheimer's disease, and those in permanent comatose states. We typically extend full moral consideration to humans in these conditions despite thinking that they may lack the capacity to have

experiences and care what happens to them. There are a variety of responses. First, in some cases the condition may be temporary and either naturally or medically changeable. Second, one might admit that these humans are no longer subjects of a life, yet, given the role that sympathy and solidarity play in human psychology and morality, it would be unwise to expel them from the moral community. Third, one could admit that marginal cases do not deserve to have *completely* equal moral consideration as non-marginal humans (we regularly restrict the rights of the those with severe mental illness), yet they do not thereby forfeit all moral consideration such that we treat them as mere objects. It should be said that marginal cases are most often invoked *by* animal welfare advocates in their attempt to point out that there is no nonarbitrary reason to exclude nonhuman sentient beings from the moral community. I have already accepted that there is no nonarbitrary reason to exclude nonhuman sentient beings from the moral community. While there is more to be said on the moral challenges presented by marginal cases, those challenges do not directly pertain to the present inquiry. For more on marginal cases and animal welfare, see Norcross 2004.

17. If one agrees with Hursthouse's virtue ethics, understanding the purposiveness of different organisms may be the most important piece of information one needs in order to construct a normative ethical system.

18. I will not take up the objection here, though I admit to being dubious how influential the practical problems associated with an expanding moral community ought to be in accepting or rejecting a moral position. No doubt the moral deliberations of most Americans were simpler when, to varying degrees, women, children, the poor, non-Europeans, infidels, and animals were denied full membership in the moral community. Should we then retract the moral community to what it was in 1850?

19. Here one could respond with a best-of-all-possible-worlds argument or some kind of theodicy. Again, I leave these issues to the theologians.

20. Thompson understands herself as refuting environmental ethics *tout court*, though by environmental ethics she means what I have described as ecocentrism. It is common in the literature for ecocentrism to become synonymous with environmental ethics. It is the ecocentrists themselves who are responsible for this, given that they frequently find other forms of nonanthropocentrism insufficiently concerned with the entire natural world. Arne Naess, who pejoratively categorizes non-ecocentric environmentalism as "shallow ecology" (in contrast to his ecocentric "deep ecology") is a prime example. So is Rolston who, as we saw, claimed that any ethic that falls short of recognizing the moral considerability of ecosystems is not a sufficiently environmental ethic.

Chapter Four

Value and Wilderness *qua* Wilderness

Two central questions of this book are: what is the value of wilderness, and what argument for wilderness preservation is possible based upon this value? Chapter 4 directly addresses the first question and prepares the way for an examination of the second in the final chapter.

Chapter 1 established and defended an understanding of wilderness essentially in agreement with 1964 Wilderness Act. Fundamentally, I am concerned with the value of wilderness *qua* wilderness rather than merely values that are, or can be, associated with wilderness. What do I mean by 'wilderness *qua* wilderness?' I mean wilderness itself: the untrammeled natural world; land retaining its primeval characteristics; parts of the earth insignificantly influenced by human activity—past or present, intentional or unintentional, conspicuous or inconspicuous. Wilderness is a condition of the natural world, and the places called 'wilderness' comprise a domain marked by this condition. In posing the question of the value of wilderness *qua* wilderness, I am asking: what is the value of a domain marked by this condition?

Inquiring into the value of wilderness *qua* wilderness is importantly distinct from, say, inquiring into the value of wilderness *qua* recreation area or wilderness *qua* biological laboratory. To be sure, wilderness does have value as a recreation area and biological laboratory. But in the value of wilderness *qua* recreation area, priority belongs to the value of recreation areas such that the value of wilderness depends upon first ascertaining the value of recreation areas, and then demonstrating the extent to which wilderness can serve in this capacity. The value of wilderness *qua* wilderness would need to be the value of the untrammeled natural world; of land retaining its primeval characteristics; of parts of the earth insignificantly influenced by human activity—past or present, intentional or unintentional, conspicuous or inconspicuous.

This chapter has four parts. The first will consider, for a final time, the extent to which an argument on behalf of wilderness preservation could be grounded in nonanthropocentric considerations. This topic was largely dealt with in chapter 2 and chapter 3, though, in the case of one argument, not directly. I will argue that extant nonanthropocentric arguments for wilderness preservation are inadequate and that no superior nonanthropocentric argument is likely to be forthcoming.

The inadequacy of nonanthropocentric considerations prompts us to look again at what anthropocentric considerations have to offer. To this end, the second part reflects on anthropocentric arguments for wilderness and the instrumental and ultimate (intrinsic value$_1$) values on which they depend. I acknowledge that there are many cogent anthropocentric arguments on behalf of wilderness; these arguments are an adequate means to achieve the ends of much contemporary environmental activism. That said, most anthropocentric arguments for wilderness preservation fail to get at the value of wilderness *qua* wilderness.

The third part identifies the unique, non-replicable value of wilderness as the value of the existence of a portion of the natural world that is not created, controlled, or significantly influenced by human beings; it is the value of a worldly other-than-human domain. I explain, with a variety of thought experiments, that this value is the one for which wilderness is a necessary condition, and why, at best, wilderness is a sufficient condition for the satisfaction of the value that ground other arguments in its defense. The fourth part of this chapter grounds these thought experiments in recent scholarship from the Breakthrough Institute. This scholarship makes the case that an increasingly artificial, human-directed biosphere is not just a flight of philosophical fancy; such a world is closer than we might think, and, for some, more desirable, a fact which adds a practical, political dimension to a debate over the value of wilderness. Additionally, this scholarship points the way to a link between bioethics and environmental ethics that will be taken up in chapter 5.

NONANTHROPOCENTRIC ARGUMENTS FOR WILDERNESS PRESERVATION

Chapter 3 discussed the emphasis that environmental philosophy has placed on establishing some form of nonanthropocentrism. If humans are the loci of all fundamental value, as anthropocentrism has it, then the value of the nonhuman world ultimately derives from us, and nature is only worth something if it is worth something to us. Nonanthropocentrism, however, denies the moral superiority of humans over other beings and does not believe that all moral deliberations should be reduced to deliberations about what is valuable for humans. It is unsurprising that environmentalists have been wary of anthropocentrism and attracted to nonanthropocentrism.

Chapter 3 also explained that one way—perhaps the surest way—to establish the nonanthropocentric value of wilderness would be to establish wilderness's intrinsic value. I reviewed four types of intrinsic value: ultimate value (intrinsic value$_1$, hereafter always referred to as ultimate value), moral considerability (intrinsic value$_2$), inherent value (intrinsic value$_3$), and value independent of valuation (intrinsic value$_4$). It is important to realize, however, that only intrinsic value in the second, third, or fourth senses could establish a form of nonanthropocentric value for wilderness.

Intrinsic value$_1$ is non-instrumental, ultimate value—my grandfather's knife has intrinsic value$_1$ inasmuch as it is, for me, valuable whether or not it is also a means to some other end. But establishing the intrinsic value$_1$ of the knife doesn't make the case for nonanthropocentrism because the locus of the value is still a human being. Similarly, establishing the intrinsic value$_1$ of wilderness would do nothing to establish a nonanthropocentric ethic; hence, the link between nonanthropocentrism and intrinsic value is dependent on a justifiable ascription of the second, third, or fourth type of intrinsic value.

I further argued that ascriptions of intrinsic value$_3$ and intrinsic value$_4$ are not justified in the case of wilderness. Additionally, I gave reasons for thinking that sentience is a necessary condition for moral considerability such that any ascription of intrinsic value$_2$ to wilderness will need to make the case that wilderness is a sentient being. Given the arguments against extending independent moral considerability to plants and ecosystems (i.e., against biocentrism and ecocentrism), I suggested that there is a strong argument *a fortiori* against the moral considerability of wilderness. So then, one conclusion drawn from chapter 3 is that the value of wilderness, whatever it might be, should be understood as some form of instrumental value or intrinsic value$_1$ or a combination of both. Still, it will be instructive to consider, one final time, the extent to which an argument for wilderness preservation could have a nonanthropocentric basis.

In "An Amalgamation of Wilderness Preservation Arguments," Michael Nelson identifies thirty "traditional and contemporary arguments proffered on behalf of 'wilderness'" (Nelson 1998, 154). It is always possible that additional arguments are lurking in the literature, but Nelson's list is the most comprehensive yet assembled. Having studied the philosophical and popular literature, his amalgamation is a broad and charitable rendering of the reasons that have been put forth in favor of wilderness.[1] I submit that every argument in defense of wilderness is grounded in some belief in the value of wilderness. These values are not always argued for, nor are they always made explicit. Nevertheless, for every argument of the form "Wilderness should be preserved because x" there must be a fundamental premise that begins "x has or embodies the value y." If, for any given argument, the y can be reasonably interpreted as nonanthropocentric, then the argument is grounded in nonanthropocentric value.

Of the arguments Nelson identifies, only three are nonanthropocentric: the Gaia hypothesis argument; the intrinsic value argument; and the animal welfare argument.[2] If one of these arguments has merit, then we are justified in continuing to hope for a nonanthropocentric basis for wilderness preservation; if not, we must see what anthropocentrism has to offer.

As it happens, we have already encountered these arguments and found each of them wanting. Chapter 2 presented and responded to the animal welfare argument, and chapter 3 took up the intrinsic value argument. Although the arguments in chapter 3 against biocentrism and ecocentrism apply, in my view, equally to the Gaia hypothesis argument, I did not explicitly present or critique the Gaia argument. The other two arguments, having already been considered at length, will be dealt with briefly.

The Gaia Hypothesis Argument

The Gaia hypothesis argument claims that earth itself is a living being, or at least tantamount to a living organism (called *Gaia* after the Greek earth goddess).[3] The argument further claims that, as a living being, the earth itself is morally considerable.[4]

Proponents of the Gaia argument rely on an argument from analogy. The earth, like a human being, appears to be a self-correcting, self-sustaining entity composed of organic systems. A human, as a living entity, depends on the functioning of its component systems: liver, kidneys, heart, etc. So too, it seems to some, Gaia depends on the functioning of her *eco*systems: forests, wetlands, oceans, etc. "Wild ecosystems," writes Nelson, "might be likened to the internal organs of a multicelled organism. . . . With Gaia, designated wilderness areas could be said to perform certain services invaluable to the smooth functioning of the earth organism . . . without a liver a human cannot live; without wilderness earth perhaps cannot either" (ibid., 188).

The Gaia argument then moves from an empirical analogy to a moral equivalency. If the earth is a living being, it deserves the same moral consideration as any other living being. And if the functioning of Gaia depends on wilderness, acknowledgment of Gaia's moral standing ought to be enough to preserve wilderness.

There are several problems with the Gaia hypothesis argument, the most fundamental of which is that it fails to give us a reason to think that the earth is alive. At best, the analogy employed results in a conditional: *if* the earth is alive, then the ecosystems might stand in relation to earth as organs stand in relation to a human being. But why think that that the earth is alive in the first place? I can admit that the earth is partially comprised of living beings, and I can further admit that these living beings are organized in self-sustaining systems. None of this, however, entails the conclusion that the earth itself it a living entity over and above its component parts.[5]

But let us suppose for the sake of argument that the earth is a living being. What does this establish? As we saw in chapter 3, it is not at all clear that simply being alive is sufficient to establish moral considerability. Gaia proponents would need an argument to establish that the earth is sentient; no such argument for sentience appears forthcoming.

Nevertheless, let us further suppose both that the earth is alive *and* that the earth is sentient and morally considerable. Even under this supposition we would not have an argument for wilderness preservation. If the earth's systems are functionally analogous to human organs (as the Gaia argument maintains), we still do not have an argument for the preservation of wild systems. A human does not need a heart and a liver; it needs something capable of circulating blood and something capable of filtering toxins. This 'something' could be a naturally occurring organ, but it could be also an artificial substitute. It is inevitable that bioengineers will one day create a pump that works better and lasts longer than the human heart. When they do, we may replace inferior hearts with new heart-like pumps as readily as we now replace inferior teeth with dental implants. So even if we accept that the earth is a living, morally considerable being (which we have no reason to accept), we do not yet have a reason to preserve wild systems. At best, we have a *pro tanto* reason to maintain systems necessary for the earth's welfare.

Let me push the critique of Gaia one step further. Imagine that the earth is alive, sentient, and *does* require the maintenance of wild systems for life. At this point, a proponent of the Gaia argument must still tell us exactly how much wilderness is required. If the earth's wild systems are indeed like human organs, then they need to be maintained practically *in toto*. We can do without one of our kidneys, but that is about it. So even granting the Gaia argument all that we have no reason to grant, we still need a nonarbitrary account that explains how much wilderness, and what kind of wilderness, the earth needs to enable its "smooth functioning." And this argument cannot merely be an explanation of how much wilderness is necessary to keep various plants and animals alive; it must speak to what will keep the earth itself alive as an independent being . . . which loops us back to the problem of establishing what it means to say that the earth is alive.

Finally, in addition to criticisms just presented, the Gaia hypothesis argument is also vulnerable to all the objections leveled against ecocentrism in chapter 3. We have ample reason, then, to rule out the possibility of establishing the nonanthropocentric value of wilderness via the Gaia hypothesis argument. It may be rhetorically provocative to say that the earth is alive, but we should understand this characterization as a metaphor and nothing more.

The Animal Welfare Argument

A version of the animal welfare argument was presented in chapter 2 (there called the AFW). Simply put, the argument states that at least some animals are morally considerable and that the destruction of wilderness is inimical to their welfare; consequently, we have a moral reason to preserve wilderness so as to avoid causing harm.[6]

The animal welfare argument is not wrong, so far as it goes. But as previously explained, it has two serious flaws. First, it relies on an unnecessary disjunction in which we either preserve wilderness as it is and promote animal welfare *or* we interfere in wilderness and do harm to animal welfare. Second, it ignores the OFW; that is, it ignores the fact that wilderness is the source of incalculable suffering for innumerable sentient beings. An implication of the OFW, argued for in chapter 2, is that if one is committed to an ethic in which the welfare of nonhuman animals matters, then one has, in many cases, a strong reason to oppose wilderness (though only in such a way that animal welfare is increased).

The Intrinsic Value Argument

The intrinsic value argument brings us once again into familiar territory.[7] I considered intrinsic value at length in chapter 3, surveying four senses of intrinsic value and arguing that intrinsic value in the second, third, and fourth senses is inapplicable in the case of wilderness. At most, then, the intrinsic value argument is an argument for intrinsic value$_1$—intrinsic value as ultimate, non-instrumental value. I have acknowledged that wilderness has such a value; I have also explained that such a value does not establish moral considerability. The intrinsic value argument fails to make the case for a nonanthropocentric defense of wilderness. (See chapter 3: "Intrinsic Value as Ultimate, Non-Instrumental Value" and "Intrinsic Value as Moral Considerability").

To summarize: there are three extant arguments for wilderness preservation that rely on the nonanthropocentric value of wilderness—the Gaia hypothesis argument, the intrinsic value argument, and the animal welfare argument. Of the three, only the animal welfare argument is compelling. But, as argued in chapter 2, an argument for wilderness based on concern for animal welfare is undermined by the OFW. As a result, I contend that an argument for wilderness preservation is best grounded in anthropocentric value.

ANTHROPOCENTRIC ARGUMENTS FOR WILDERNESS PRESERVATION

There is a plethora of anthropocentric arguments in defense of wilderness. These arguments appeal to wilderness's instrumental value as well its ultimate value. I see no reason to doubt that the extant anthropocentric arguments are currently sufficient for the purposes of conservation, preservation, and various other forms of environmental activism. If one's goal is to arrest the destruction of wilderness, the appeals to enlightened self-interest popularized by the Sierra Club, Rachel Carson, and Al Gore are equal to the task. Indeed, any one of the twenty-seven anthropocentric arguments in Nelson's amalgamation provides a good reason to preserve the wilderness.[8]

All of the anthropocentric arguments are grounded in something of value to or for human beings, but the value is of two kinds: instrumental and ultimate. A thing has value instrumentally if it serves as a means to an end, if it is merely a tool enabling one to access some other thing of value. The knife in my kitchen is instrumentally valuable; it is a tool that helps me to prepare meals, the eating of which I value. So while the knife has value, I must look beyond the knife to explain the value. A thing has ultimate value if it is itself an end rather than a means. My grandfather's knife is of ultimate value inasmuch as the value does not rely on whether or not it can successfully provide access to some other valuable thing; I get value from the knife itself.

There is a potential problem with the distinction between instrumental and ultimate value as I have just explained it. I said that the kitchen knife has instrumental value because I do not value the knife itself but only the way it helps me prepare meals, and let us suppose that I value the meals because they arrest hunger pains, give me feelings of pleasure, and sustain my conscious state. I then said that my grandfather's knife has ultimate value because I value that knife for itself, not as a means to an end. But is that true? What is it about my grandfather's knife that I value? I value the way it reminds me of my grandfather; I value the craftsmanship; I value the way it makes me feel part of a tradition. Though I say that I value the knife itself, it may be that I value the knife because I value the conscious states it engenders, or that I value the experience of these states. But notice that the same can be said of the kitchen knife. So why can I say that my grandfather's knife has ultimate rather than instrumental value? And how is it that the instrumental/ ultimate distinction I am using is one that most of us employ—and employ successfully, without difficulty or confusion—in our everyday lives if it seems to break down so quickly?

Chapter 3's "Intrinsic Value as Ultimate, Non-Instrumental Value" flagged the tricky metaethical issue of what thing or things can have ultimate value, and the question of whether all ultimate value must reduce to a single source. If, for example, one was to conclude that all value reduces to the value of certain desirable conscious states and experiences then *everything* save for these desirable states and experiences would be of instrumental value.[9] In "Intrinsic Value as Ultimate, Non-Instrumental Value," I said that I did not need to engage with this debate. It is possible to explain why we can and do meaningfully talk about a thing like my grandfather's knife as a source of ultimate value and talk about a thing like the kitchen knife as a source of instrumental value without waiting on a verdict from metaethics concerning the final source (or sources) of all ultimate value.

Perhaps the reason it is possible to meaningfully use the instrumental/ultimate distinction has to do with causation, specifically where a thing stands in a given causal chain of value. Even supposing that all value reduces to some desirable experience or conscious state, my grandfather's knife is the direct cause of the valuable experiences and conscious states; the kitchen knife, however, is several causal links down the chain. I may value a kitchen knife because it helps in preparing meals, and I may the value the meals because I value the experience of eating, but in that case it is the meal that has ultimate value, as the meal is the source (in the sense of being the proximate cause) of that which I value. Even if I only value my grandfather's knife because I value the conscious states it engenders, it is importantly different from the way I value a kitchen knife: my grandfather's knife is the necessary, sufficient, and immediate (or constitutive) condition of my valuing it, whereas I could value a kitchen knife without *that* particular knife being a necessary, sufficient and immediate (constitutive) condition of my doing so—any other kitchen knife could do because the particular knife itself is not the locus of the value.

This meaningful distinction between instrumental and ultimate value applies equally well to the various anthropocentric values of wilderness such that I see no problem in continuing to speak of wilderness as a source of instrumental value *and* a source of ultimate value. Rather than review all the many anthropocentric arguments for wilderness preservation, I will illustrate the value of wilderness with two such arguments from instrumental value and two from ultimate value.[10]

Instrumental and Ultimate Value in Wilderness

Most arguments for wilderness preservation are grounded in wilderness's allegedly anthropocentric instrumental value. Two prominent examples are the natural resources argument and the social bonding argument (Nelson 1998, 156–57, 185–86).

The natural resources argument locates the reason for wilderness preservation in the "significant qualities of untapped yet precious physical resources" that it contains (ibid., 156). Most of us are familiar with some version of this argument. Spoil the wilderness and we might spoil the potentially valuable resources therein, whether these resources are for present or future use. Wilderness is a source of food, building supplies, and medicine; food, building supplies, and medicine are of value to human beings; therefore, wilderness is of value to human beings.

The social bonding argument maintains that excursions into the wilderness facilitates social bonding between human groups such as families, friends, colleagues, and neighbors. "Because, and to the extent that, we are social animals and our continued survival depends on effective social interaction," writes Nelson, "we ought to value social bonding. Exposure to 'wilderness' is thought to intensify experience and provide a vector for high-level and successful interpersonal cohesion" (ibid., 186). The argument is that social bonding improves social interaction, and improved social interaction increases our chance of survival (and presumably our welfare); wilderness facilitates social bonding; therefore, wilderness is valuable.

As stated, the natural resources argument and the social bonding argument are but two of many arguments for wilderness preservation premised on the instrumental value of wilderness. All other such arguments, however, follow the same logic. A particular feature of wilderness is identified as valuable because of the way it leads, sooner or later, to something humans consider to be of ultimate value.

Not all anthropocentric arguments for wilderness preservation appeal to wilderness's instrumental value. Some are based upon the value of wilderness as an end in itself, as a source of ultimate value rather than a means to some other valuable end. Two examples are the art gallery argument and the mental therapy argument.

The art gallery argument (ibid., 166–67) places the value of a wilderness in the value of the aesthetic experiences it provides. Experiences of the beautiful and the sublime are a familiar component of wilderness excursions, and those who value such experiences often look to the wilderness for satisfaction. Aesthetic experience is frequently cited as a paradigmatic example of ultimate value. The notion of *l'art pour l'art* relies on the belief that art, in it purest form, is an end in itself rather than a means. So, too, the beauty of the wilderness—a frequent object of artistic representation—is taken to be an end in itself. The art gallery argument takes wilderness to be of ultimate value because it takes the aesthetic experience of the wilderness (co-constituted by the wilderness) to be of ultimate value.

The mental therapy argument (ibid., 164–66) follows the same reasoning exchanging aesthetic experience for psychological health.[11] "Wilderness advocates have often claimed," writes Nelson, "that what are taken to be wilderness experiences can be psychologically therapeutic and can even significantly help treat psychologically disturbed persons" (ibid., 164). So the wilderness has ultimate value, and ought to be preserved, inasmuch as it can directly benefit our mental health.

In offering précises of the natural resource, social bonding, art gallery, and mental therapy arguments, I am attempting neither to endorse nor refute them. Readers can make up their own minds as to the arguments' merits and demerits. I use them here simply to illustrate some of the variety of anthropocentric arguments for wilderness preservation, and the way in which these arguments can be grouped according to whether they appeal to the wilderness's instrumental or ultimate value.

Some may still be bothered by the instrumental/ultimate distinction itself, feeling that even something like the art gallery argument relies on the way we can use wilderness as means to some end, the end in this case a certain kind of aesthetic experience. Or perhaps one is inclined to agree with a certain pragmatic view of value that takes all values to be instrumental and linked in a mutually supporting web (see Weston 1985, 337). Alternatively, one may question the validity of an infinite regress argument, which argues for the existence of ultimate value on the grounds that instrumental value makes no sense without it (see Jamieson 2008, 72–73). These are important lines of inquiry, and I do not mean to dismiss them. However, in presenting the intrinsic/ultimate distinction, and showing how it pertains to arguments for wilderness preservation, I am only reporting how certain conceptions of value have been used in the wilderness debate.

THE VALUE OF WILDERNESS *QUA* WILDERNESS

The extant anthropocentric arguments for wilderness preservation are ethically compelling and politically motivating from the standpoint of environmental activism. Philosophically, however, they have a common shortcoming: none are grounded in the value of wilderness *qua* wilderness. The values to which the arguments appeal, whether instrumental or ultimate, are in fact not unique to wilderness, which is to say that wilderness is perhaps a sufficient condition for the enjoyment of the value in question, but it is not a necessary one. The value on which these arguments rely does not itself rely on the existence of wilderness.[12]

Consider the arguments of the preceding section. The wilderness is a sufficient source for the provision of certain natural resources, but it is not a necessary source. Timber, for example, can be farmed, and diamonds can be created in laboratories. At the present moment, wilderness may be the best source for various natural resources, but this fact does not amount to a physical or logical dependency upon *wilderness* for these resources. The only thing for which wilderness is a necessary source is wilderness. The same holds for the social bonding, art gallery, and mental therapy arguments (and every other argument collected by Nelson). In each case wilderness is a sufficient condition for the provision of a certain value, but not a necessary one. Social bonding does not require untrammeled land; aesthetic satisfaction is not dependent upon the natural world retaining its primeval characteristics; stable mental health surely has other sources.

One might point out that while wilderness is not a necessary condition for natural resources or social bonding or aesthetic experiences, it *is* a necessary condition for *wild* natural resources, and *wild* social bonding experiences, and *wild* beauty. In the absence of wilderness, none of these values is realizable.

Such a response, however, is either a tautology or it begs the question against the value of wilderness. If we change the social bonding argument to say that bonding experiences in the wilderness are only possible in the presence of wilderness, the statement is vacuous. If we change the argument to say that bonding experiences in the wilderness are uniquely valuable by virtue of taking place in the wilderness, we are arguing that wilderness is valuable because it enables wilderness bonding experiences, and that wilderness bonding experiences are valuable because they take place in the wilderness. At best, such a move would demonstrate the need for an examination of wilderness *qua* wilderness such that we could better understand why *wild* experiences seem to us uniquely valuable—which is precisely what we need to consider.

Imagine a world in which the term 'wilderness' no longer has a referent. Call it world-X. In world-X there is no part of nature that can be reasonably called 'wild'; everything that exists is artificial. Suppose, however, that world-X is sensorially and functionally equivalent to our own world. By sensorially equivalent I mean that world-X looks, smells, sounds, feels and tastes exactly like our world. By functionally equivalent, I mean that world-X can do everything that our world could do without any observable difference, and can do so such that world-X functions and will continue to function in a way that makes it indistinguishable from our world.

As stipulated, there can be no wilderness areas in world-X, yet the world must appear and function as if there were; as a result, everything that comprises the wilderness in our world has an artificial analogue in world-X. The 'wild' parts of world-X are full of biomechanical tigers that produce biomechanical cubs who learn to hunt biomechanical prey. Artificial trees release oxygen and absorb carbon dioxide. The slopes of the Matterhorn are as perilous as ever, but the rock was manufactured in a factory outside Zurich, and remotely controlled clouds distribute artificial snow. If these examples feel too silly for serious engagement, imagine some other means of removing wilderness from world-X while keeping it sensorially and functionally equivalent to our world such that a resident of Earth suddenly transported to world-X would be unable to tell the difference. And yet there *is* a difference. Everything in world-X is either human-created or human-controlled or both; one way or another, everything in this world bears the intentional mark of humanity.

World-X is unsettling, yet it is difficult to say precisely why. The thirty arguments for wilderness preservation assembled by Nelson are not helpful. For any argument citing the instrumental value of wilderness (e.g., the natural resources argument, the pharmacopoeia argument, the defense of democracy argument), we can understand world-X as providing the same sort of instrumental values. For any argument citing the ultimate, non-instrumental value of wilderness (e.g., the art gallery argument, the mental therapy argument, the life support argument), we can also understand world-X as being an equivalent source. Remember, world-X is sensorially and functionally equivalent to our world.

We can even imagine that world-X is equipped with a perfected version of Robert Nozick's experience machine.[13] The experience machine is a fanciful device capable of providing an individual with any possible experience. Moreover, once an individual enters the machine, she is no longer aware that she is in the machine but believes that the things she is experiencing are really happening. With the addition of the experience machine, any argument for the preservation of wilderness that is grounded in the value of an experience that wilderness can supply may no longer be compelling to a resident of world-X.

The experience machine helps to show a potential shortcoming of arguments for wilderness preservation that are not grounded in the value of wilderness *qua* wilderness, but it can also help us see what is so unsettling about world-X. Nozick introduces the experience machine to show that desirable experiences are not all that matter to us. If they were, anyone offered entry to an experience machine scenario should be rushing to get in. As it happens, very few people are attracted by the idea of permanently entering an experience machine or even entering it for extended periods of time.[14] The reasons for this, suggests Nozick, are that human beings care about doing, being, and reality.

We don't just want the *experience* of climbing mountains; we want to *climb* mountains. But climbing mountains is not possible in the machine; all that is possible in the machine is the experience of climbing mountains. One of the reasons we want to do things, thinks Nozick, rather than just have the experience of doing them, is that we want to *be* a certain kind of person—say, a courageous person. How do we become a courageous person? By doing courageous things. But merely having the experience of doing courageous things in the machine (the tank, as Nozick calls it) won't make one courageous. "Someone floating in the tank is an indeterminate blob," writes Nozick. If we accept the idea that who we are is in some significant way determined by what we do, and if we realize that we cannot *do* anything in the machine, then "There is no answer to the question of what a person is like who has long been in the tank. Is he courageous, kind, intelligent, witty, loving? It's not merely that it's difficult to tell; there no way he is" (Nozick 2015, 28).

Why, though, do we care about *really* doing things and *really* being a certain kind of person rather than simply having the experience of doing and being whatever and whoever we want? Nozick suggests we have a fundamental respect and desire for a reality that is independent of human reality. "Plugging into an experience machine," he writes, "limits us to a man-made reality. . . . There is no *actual* contact with any deeper reality, though the experience of it can be simulated. . . . We learn that something matters to us in addition to experience by imagining an experience machine and then realizing that we would not use it" (ibid., 28–29).

World-X is capable of providing every valuable good and every valuable experience to which arguments for wilderness preservation typically appeal. I do not suppose, however, that a single wilderness enthusiast would be interested in swapping our world for world-X. The reason is that there is, in fact, one type of good and one type of experience that world-X still cannot provide: it cannot provide goods or experiences that are actually *wild*. Just like the experience machine, world-X is unsettling for the way in which it limits us to a man-made reality and cuts us off from a world that is other-than-human *even if* such a world is sensorially and functionally equivalent our own. Intuitively and fundamentally, we find wilderness, as a worldly domain of the other-than-human, to be valuable *as* a domain of the other-than-human. The reflections of Edward Abbey and Bill McKibben illustrate the point.[15]

Abbey, a lover of the desert wilderness of the American Southwest, struggled to understand his attraction to such a dangerous and inhospitable place. Why seek out the wilderness, he wondered? An answer came to him while hiking in a particularly desolate spot in northern Arizona. He looked out from the top of one mesa and saw "more canyons, more mesas and plateaus, more mountains, more cloud-dappled sun-spangled leagues of desert sand and desert rock. . . . There was nothing out there. Nothing at all. Nothing but the desert. Nothing but the silent world" (Abbey 1977, 21). Roderick Nash explains that in looking at nothing, Abbey realized he was in fact looking at something extremely valuable. The value, says Nash, "had to do with the emptiness and otherness and the way that wilderness was the antipode of civilization and all its myths, including those concerning wilderness" (Nash 2014, 270). Wilderness wasn't valuable despite its otherness, despite its lack of civilization; it was valuable because of these features.

Bill McKibben seconds Abbey's intuition when he expresses fear over the possibility of increased human control of the natural world. "How, if the seasons are no longer inevitable, can we accept the inevitability, and even the beauty, of death?" (McKibben 1990: 83). McKibben shares a story that illustrates how his valuation of nature is dependent upon it remaining free from human influence. Hiking to a waterfall he has visited in the past, he recalls how its power and beauty once filled him with a sense of awe at what nature can do. His current visit is different, though, given that he no longer sees the gushing water as a work of nature but as the unintentional by-product of anthropogenic climate change.

> But as I sat there this time, and thought about the dry summer we'd just come through, there was nothing awe-inspiring or instructive, or even lulling, in the fall of the water. It suddenly seemed less like a waterfall than like a spillway to accommodate the overflow of a reservoir. That didn't decrease its beauty, but it changed its meaning. Instead of a world where rain had an independent and mysterious existence, the rain had become a subset of human activity. . . . The rain bore a brand; it was a steer, not a deer. And that was where the loneliness came from. There's nothing there except us. There's no such thing as nature anymore—that other world that isn't business and art and breakfast is now not another world, and there is nothing except us alone. (Ibid., 89)

Abbey and McKibben convey the idea that there is, in fact, just one value for which wilderness is a necessary condition, and that this value is that of wilderness itself: a domain that fundamentally was, is, and will be other-than-human. Dale Jamieson observes that the value of the something else, the other, is not conditional on its caring for or taking a personal interest in human beings. He further suggests that one reason the wilderness can be so comforting is because is does *not* care about us. Like McKibben, Jamieson notes "a kind of loneliness about life in an environment that you dominate." Aside from its many instrumental uses, part of what we value about the wilderness "is that she 'does her own thing' and is largely indifferent to us." It is precisely the indifference that is "a welcome relief from life in the human-dominated world" (Jamieson 2008, 166). In a world devoid of wilderness, no such sanctuary would exist, and no such relief would be possible.

THOUGHT EXPERIMENTS AND AN ARTIFICIAL WORLD

The thought experiments in "The Value of Wilderness *qua* Wilderness" push us to consider what would be lost in a world devoid of wilderness. What we find is that, in such a world, we would essentially and necessarily lose one thing: a worldly domain of the other-than-human; places and states of affairs neither created nor controlled by human beings.

Philosophers disagree about the usefulness of thought experiments. Some philosophers are averse to them, perhaps because certain experiments stretch credulity, or appear self-serving, or because they threaten to trivialize matters of grave practical import.[16] I find thought experiments a useful philosophical tool with a long, productive history. We call Plato's account of the Ring of Gyges a myth but it is the paradigm of a thought experiment (and quite a good one). Nevertheless, almost everyone agrees that the more believable the proposed scenario, the more effective a thought experiment is likely to be. Recently a group of philosophers, sociologists, economists, biologists, environmentalists, and policy experts writing for the Breakthrough Institute have given reason to think that the idea of an increasingly artificial, human-managed natural world, is not as far-fetched as it might initially appear.

The Breakthrough Institute, founded in 2003 by environmental policy experts Ted Nordhaus and Michael Schellenberger, is a "global research center that identifies and promotes technological solutions to environmental and human development challenges" (Breakthrough 2018). The founders gained notoriety in 2004 with their treatise *The Death of Environmentalism*. In this work they argue that traditional models of environmental conservation and preservation are bankrupt, and that, going forward, environmentalists ought to embrace rather than oppose technology and innovation, and that capitalism and big business—the traditional bogeymen of environmentalism—need to be seen as partners in any realistic global environmental strategy (Nordhaus and Schellenberger 2004). Especially germane to the present inquiry is the fact that many scholars affiliated with the Breakthrough Institute argue that increased human control over the natural world is inevitable, desirable, or both.

Sociologist and anthropologist Bruno Latour is the Breakthrough Institute's most eloquent spokesman, and his essay "Love Your Monsters: Why We Must Care for Our Technologies as We Do Our Children" is the clearest expression of the "post-environmental" thinking it endorses (Latour 2012). In the essay, Latour asks us to reconsider the lesson of Mary Shelley's *Frankenstein*. On one reading of the novel—let's call it the traditional reading—*Frankenstein* is a cautionary tale warning modern man to check his hubris and not meddle too deeply with nature. The scientific revolution of the seventeenth century and the Enlightenment of eighteenth century left humanity more powerful than ever before. Secrets of nature, cloaked in mystery for millennia, began yielding at an unprecedented rate to the penetrating application of microscopes and telescopes and the critical application of logic and reason. In the novel, young Victor Frankenstein harnesses the new learning in an attempt to conquer death itself. The result is the creation of a monster. On the traditional reading, Frankenstein's sin is the use of science and reason to create the monster, or, less prejudicially, to create that which he should not have created. On Latour's reading, Dr. Frankenstein didn't necessarily sin in bringing his creation to life; he sinned in bringing it to life and then failing to care for it.

Latour uses Frankenstein's monster as a metaphor for all technology and innovation. The creature isn't created a monster—it becomes a monster when its creator abandons it to the world. Monstrous consequences are the potential of all new technologies; our mistake is not creating them, but in refusing to properly care for them. In the case of humanity's mastery and manipulation of nature, "It is not that we have failed to care for Creation," as much traditional environmentalism maintains, "but that we have failed to care for our technological creations."

> The goal of political ecology must not be to stop innovating, inventing, creating, and intervening. The real goal must be to have the same type of patience and commitment to our creations as God the Creator, Himself. And the comparison is not blasphemous: we have taken the whole of Creation on our shoulders and have become coextensive with the Earth. (Ibid., Introduction)

Latour rejects the idea that there is something intrinsically misguided in striving to achieve the sort of mastery and progress envisioned by proponents of the scientific revolution and the Enlightenment. "Why," he asks, "do we suddenly feel so frightened at the moment that our dreams of modernization finally come true? Why do we suddenly turn pale and wish to fall back on the other side of Hercules's columns, thinking we are being punished for having transgressed the sign: 'Thou shall not transgress?'" (ibid., section 1). For Latour, we have little to fear from technology and innovation so long as we think carefully about our creations before creating them, and then proceed to care for them in the way that good parents ought to care for their children, however ill-tempered and imperfect those children turn out to be. In short, we will be all right so long as we avoid Dr. Frankenstein's real mistake: not a hubristic meddling in nature, but a failure to love his monster.

In "Conservation and the Anthropocene," Peter Kareiva, Michelle Marvier, and Robert Lalasz echo Latour's thesis and argue that it ought to be applied to matters of conservation now that we have entered a new geological epoch defined by human influence on the planet.[17] "Scientists," they report, "have coined a name for our era—the Anthropocene—to emphasize that we have entered a new geological era in which humans dominate every flux and cycle of the planet's ecology and geochemistry."

Most people worldwide (regardless of culture) welcome the opportunities that development provides to improve lives of grinding rural poverty. At the same time, the global scale of this transformation has reinforced conservation's intense nostalgia for wilderness and a past of pristine nature. But conservation's continuing focus upon preserving islands of Holocene ecosystems in the age of the Anthropocene is both anachronistic and counterproductive. (Kareiva, Marvier, Lalasz 2012, Section 3)

The authors find it ironic that Anthropocene conservation "is losing the war to protect nature despite winning one of its hardest fought battle—to create parks, game preserves, and wilderness areas." They point out that we are "losing species at an alarming rate" despite 13% of the earth's landmass—an area the size of South America—already being "protected."[18] In place of traditional conservation or preservation, they advocate for "a new vision of a planet in which nature—forest, wetlands, diverse species, and other ancient ecosystems—exists amid a wide variety of modern, human landscapes" (ibid., Introduction).

Kareiva, Marvier, and Lalasz are keen to rebut the traditional narrative of impending anthropogenic environmental collapse. Nature is far more resilient and adaptive than most realize, they argue, and the idea that all life hangs in some precarious balance, an ecological house of cards ready to fold at the slightest touch of a human hand, is more fear mongering than good science. The American chestnut, the passenger pigeon, the Steller's sea cow, the dodo: all "went extinct, along with countless other species . . . with no catastrophic or even measurable effects." "Nature," they say, "is so resilient that it can recover rapidly from even the most powerful human disturbances." The wildlife around Chernobyl is thriving, and "in the Bikini Atoll, the site of multiple nuclear bomb tests . . . the number of coral species has actually increased relative to before the explosion." They observe that much has been made of the collapse of the cod industry in the Georges Bank; by contrast, they do not find it surprising that little is said about the fact that the "biomass of cod has recovered to precollapse levels" given that the resiliency of nature "does not play well to an audience somehow addicted to stories of collapse and environmental apocalypse" (ibid., section 2).

Erle Ellis, professor of environmental science at the University of Maryland, agrees that we are indeed living in a new geological epoch—the Anthropocene—in which "humans have become the dominant force on the planet" (Ellis 2012, Introduction). And like Latour, Kareiva, Marvier, and Lalasz, he does not see this as a harbinger of doom. He urges us to accept "that the human enterprise has continued to expand beyond natural limits for millennia. Indeed, the history of human civilization might be characterized as a history of transgressing our natural limits and thriving" (ibid., section

4). Ellis sounds like a traditional environmentalist when he proclaims "The Earth we have inherited from our ancestors is now our responsibility," but the comparison ends there. He continues:

> Our powers may yet exceed our ability to manage them but there is no alternative except to shoulder the mantle of planetary stewardship. A good, or at least a better, Anthropocene is within our grasp. Creating that future will mean going beyond fears of transgressing natural limits and nostalgic hopes of returning to some pastoral or pristine state. (Ibid., section 4)

A common theme connects ideas from the Breakthrough Institute: since we already live in a geological epoch defined by human intervention, let us accept that the right kind of human intervention can help rather than harm the environment, and let us not shy away from using all the scientific and technological ingenuity we can muster to improve the human situation. While none of the authors cited are specifically concerned with wilderness *qua* wilderness, two things are clear: (1) they can envision a world devoid of anything that could meaningfully be called wilderness; and (2) such a world doesn't bother them. For them, the idea of pristine nature or wilderness is, at best, nostalgia, whereas the idea of a global future conceived, created, and controlled by humans is one toward which we should strive. Ellis summarizes the point in the concluding line of "The Planet of No Return: Human Resilience on an Artificial Planet": "Most of all, we must not see the Anthropocene as a crisis, but as the beginning of a new geological epoch ripe with *human-directed opportunity*" (ibid., emphasis added).

CONCLUSION

Many ideas coming from the Breakthrough Institute are environmentally and academically heterodox, but they cannot be dismissed as the work of a lunatic fringe. These ideas are sourced from respected scholars and professionals in the fields of sociology, environmental science, public policy, conservation biology, economics, and philosophy. None of these scholars envisions a future as extreme as world-X (that was, after all, just a thought experiment), but they do envision a future of environmental health, ecological sustainability, and economic productivity without wilderness areas and without seeing any necessity for them to exist. World-X is not on the horizon, but a world of increased artificiality and decreased wilderness may very well be. Consequently, the investigation of the value of wilderness *qua* wilderness has a contemporary practical importance that may not be obvious.

I submit that every anthropocentric value derivable from wilderness is, in principle, derivable from another source except for the value of the existence of wilderness *qua* wilderness. The values that depend on wilderness's ability to provide us with certain goods (such as the value in the natural resources argument) might be equally satisfied by artificial goods, or goods obtainable through the artificial manipulation of wilderness (e.g., tree farms). The values that depend on wilderness's ability to furnish certain experiences (such as the value of the art gallery and social bonding arguments) can, in principle, be secured through any other source capable of replicating the experience. The only valuable goods not replaceable would be those goods that are valuable *because* they are wild, and the only experiences not replicable would be those valuable *because* they derive from the wilderness. An artificial world can never generate actual contact with what Nozick calls "deeper reality," what I have been discussing as a domain of the other-than-human. To the extent that we value contact with, or even the simple existence of, such a domain, then we value wilderness *qua* wilderness.

In chapter 5, I will suggest that such a valuation admits both a secular and spiritual interpretation such that arguments in defense of wilderness *qua* wilderness might be couched in both secular and spiritual terms. I will also begin to explore whether either type of valuation—secular or spiritual—can ground a defense of wilderness capable of rebuffing the argument for the augmentation of wilderness presented in the OFW.

NOTES

1. These are not necessarily Nelson's own arguments, nor should he be taken as endorsing them.

2. One could interpret the life-support argument (Nelson 1998, 161) as anthropocentric *and* nonanthropocentric, in which case there would be four nonanthropocentric arguments. The life-support argument holds that the maintenance of wild ecosystems may be essential to the sustenance of human life on this planet, and that we can never be sure which seemingly benign human interference will set off catastrophic ecological disaster impacting human and nonhuman species. So assuming this argument has merit (though chapter 4's "Thought Experiments and an Artificial World" casts doubt on such an assumption), it may have relevance to the survival of nonhuman species as well; as such, I take it to be a part of the animal welfare argument inasmuch as a being's survival is a significant component of its welfare.

3. See Nelson 1998, 188.

4. The Gaia hypothesis argument loses force if the earth is merely tantamount to a living being, that is, if the earth is alive in a metaphorical sense only. I will therefore consider the argument under the assumption that the earth is alive rather than tantamount to being alive.

5. The Gaia hypothesis argument is reminiscent of the deistic argument from design criticized by Hume in *Dialogues Concerning Natural Religion*. Like the argument from design, the Gaia hypothesis focuses on one weak point of analogy and ignores an indefinite number of points of disanalogy. And like the argument from design, the Gaia argument seems not to notice that, should its analogy hold, it may not lead to the conclusion its proponents desire. If we admit the earth has a designer, says Hume, will must still ask why, based on what we observe, we should not also assume that our earth is the shoddy first attempt of some infant deity. Likewise, proponents of the Gaia hypothesis will have to consider the possibility that if the earth is alive, it might be a dangerous, mutant organism responsible for more suffering than satisfaction (see Hume 2017, 24–26). For a discussion of the use, and misuse, of arguments from analogy in environmental ethics see Turner 2005.

6. See Nelson 199, 186–87.

7. See Nelson 1998, 191–93.

8. It would be more accurate to say twenty-six anthropocentric arguments. The twenty-ninth argument Nelson presents is called the 'unknown and indirect benefits argument' (Nelson 1998, 190). Charitably, we might understand it as a version of the precautionary principle, cautioning us not to disrupt wilderness until we have overwhelming evidence that our disruption will not have undesirable effects. I have accepted this position and acknowledged it in the OFW. Taken at face value, however, the argument assumes that wilderness preservation will preserve whatever unknown and indirect benefits of wilderness may exist, and that humans and nonhumans could be the beneficiaries. But this is essentially an appeal to ignorance. Imagine that a deadly virus is sweeping through the population. There is a clear reason why we should find a way to stop it. But then someone points out that perhaps the virus has unknown or indirect benefits of which we are still ignorant. We do not then let the virus spread once it is in our power to arrest it. Appeals to ignorance are fallacious.

9. I am using desirable conscious states and experiences as a representative example of something to which all other value might be reduced. But it is only an example. I do not endorse this view, and the point might be made equally well with regard to freedom or beauty or the will to power or the Form of the Good or some other candidate for the fundamental source of value.

10. I am not suggesting that a thing cannot be valued both instrumentally and ultimately. My grandfather's knife becomes instrumentally valuable when I use it to whittle kindling for a fire, but it does not thereby cede its ultimate value. Further, to say that a thing is valued as an end in itself and not as a means to some other end is not to imply that it must be the end for which other things or states of affairs are the means. X may be a necessary condition for constituting the experience of y's ultimate value, but that is not the same as saying that x stands in a clear means-ends relationship with y: I can enjoy a painting without understanding light as a means to the ultimate end of my aesthetic experiences, while still recognizing that light is partially constitutive of the experience of that which is of ultimate value to me. It may be that some ultimate values of wilderness are better described as being partially constituted by things or states of affairs which are not themselves mere means to the ultimate

value, but I do not see that this will affect my argument going forward, especially my argument concerning the anthropocentric value of wilderness in relation to the OFW.

11. Psychological health can be understood as both instrumentally and ultimately valuable. If you value your mental health only because it helps you succeed at work, then you value it instrumentally. But good health (of any kind) is often valuable for its own sake. Here I take mental health to be valuable independent of its ancillary benefits.

12. Nelson mentions this shortcoming in his critique of certain arguments for wilderness preservation (Nelson 1998, 165, 167, 173, 178). I believe he does not go far enough inasmuch as he fails to acknowledge that wilderness can only be a necessary condition for an argument based entirely on the value of wilderness *qua* wilderness.

13. Nozick introduced the experience machine in his 1974 work of political philosophy *Anarchy, State, and Utopia* for reasons having nothing to do with environmental philosophy.

14. An exception might be people leading lives of significant pain, sadness, and misery; lives that on balance contain far more unhappiness than happiness; lives in which suffering is intense, unremitting, non-beneficial, unjust, and unchosen. If one's experiences are of this kind and show no sign of improving, one might readily substitute a miserable reality for an unreality of desirable experiences.

15. What I am describing as the value of wilderness *qua* wilderness resembles, in some ways, the concept of the sublime as it appears in Mendelssohn and Kant. This is perhaps unsurprising given that both authors see wild nature as a source of the experience of the sublime. Mendelssohn's sublime can be found in "The unfathomable world of the sea, a far-reaching plain, the innumerable legions of stars, every height and depth that is beyond the reach of the eye, eternity, and other such objects of nature which appear immeasurable to the senses," all of which "arouse the sort of sentiment which in several instances . . . is quite alluring, but in many cases is upsetting" (Mendelssohn 1997, 193). Kant observes that the mind is "not merely attracted" by the sublime object "but is ever being alternately repelled" such that "the sublime does not so much involve a positive pleasure as admiration or respect" (Kant 1994, 114). Alluring but upsetting; attracting while also repelling; engendering respect but not necessarily pleasure: such is the experience of wilderness. Kant's dynamical sublime can be experienced in wild nature precisely because wild nature's "immensity," the "magnitude of its *realm*," and the "irresistibility of its might . . . discloses to us a faculty of judging independently of and a superiority over nature," despite knowing that we as individuals "might have to submit to this dominion" (ibid., 120). I argue that the value of wilderness *qua* wilderness is not attainable even in something like Nozick's experience machine precisely because the value in question is dependent on wilderness's status as a domain of the other-than-human, a domain exceeding our control. It may be that experiences of the sublime would be similarly unavailable in the machine, in which case wilderness may in fact be a necessary condition for the experience of something like Kant's dynamical sublime. To the extent that experiences of the sublime are valuable, there is space for an aesthetic defense of wilderness *qua* wilderness. While much more needs to be said on the connection between wilderness and the sublime, I do not think it greatly affects my overall argument. Even if

the value of wilderness is tantamount to the value of the sublime such that wilderness is established as a necessary condition for the satisfaction of this value, I cannot see how the anthropocentric value of an experience of the sublime will generate a reason strong enough to override the nonanthropocentric moral reason to oppose wilderness generated by the OFW. Much more is said on the value of wilderness *qua* wilderness and the OFW in chapter 5.

16. I have heard some philosophers deride thought experiments as a symptom of what is wrong with analytic philosophy, a discipline so detached from the so-called real world as to be of little value to so-called real people. Such criticism strikes me as a symptom of unhelpful intramural philosophical discord. All thought experiments have limitations, and some simply aren't much good, but it would better to evaluate them case by case than to slight an entire school of philosophy from which they are perceived to emanate.

17. Kareiva is the former director of the Institute of Environment and Sustainability at UCLA and the current President and CEO of the Aquarium of the Pacific. Marvier is a professor in the Department of Environmental Studies and Sciences at Santa Clara University. Lalasz was the director of science communications at The Nature Conservancy and is the founder and CEO of Science+Story.

18. This figure is disputed, and Kareiva, Marvier, and Lalasz acknowledge that 13 percent is a high estimate.

Chapter Five

To Be or Not to Be Prometheus

In chapter 2, I used the OFW to argue that the suffering of millions of sentient creatures provides a *pro tanto* reason to oppose wilderness preservation. The opposition to wilderness preservation need not manifest itself as a wanton, self-interested, anthropocentric destruction of the natural world. Instead, the OFW is a *pro tanto* reason in favor of a limited anthropogenic augmentation of wilderness if, because, and only to the extent that it would lessen the suffering of morally considerable beings without causing greater or equivalent present or future harm. I also claimed that a rejection of the OFW would require (a) an account of the value of wilderness, (b) an argument for preservation grounded in this value, and finally (c) a belief that the value of preserving wilderness supersedes the value generated by augmenting it for the purposes of the OFW.

In chapters 3 and 4 I defended the following two assertions. First, when considering the value of wilderness, neither moral considerability (intrinsic value$_2$), nor inherent value (intrinsic value$_3$), nor value in the absence of valuers (intrinsic value$_4$) is relevant. The only relevant conceptions of value are instrumental value and ultimate value, and these are relevant only on an anthropocentric basis. Second, a fundamental defense of wilderness must be grounded in the value of wilderness *qua* wilderness rather than one of the many values for which wilderness is an instrumental source or a sufficient but not a necessary condition. If the value derived from wilderness is, in principle, derivable from some other source, then wilderness is only valuable as a source of, or as a means to, some other valuable thing. For example, the natural resources argument values wilderness as a source of goods and services beneficial to human beings; however, should humans no longer require or desire these resources, or should we find superior, artificial replacements, the natural resources argument will be significantly weakened because the value in which it is grounded is satisfiable by other means. A defense of wilderness grounded in the value of wilderness *qua* wilderness, however, would be premised on the belief that there is some value for which wilderness is a unique source, a necessary condition. An entailment of these two assertions is that a rejection of the OFW must rely on an argument grounded in the anthropocentric value of wilderness *qua* wilderness. Because the OFW merely advocates a limited human intervention in the nonhuman natural world for the purposes of lessening suffering, opposition to the OFW must explain why even such a limited intervention would, in principle, be wrong.

Chapter 4 argued that the value of wilderness *qua* wilderness is the value of the existence of a worldly domain that is neither created, controlled, or substantially affected by human beings. But why should the existence of such a domain matter to us, and what kind of argument in defense of wilderness could be built upon such a value? And can the *pro tanto* moral reason to oppose wilderness generated by the OFW be counteracted by an argument grounded in such a value?

I propose to address these questions in two ways. First, I will make a philosophical parallel between environmental ethics and bioethics. Specifically, I consider the extent to which Michael Sandel's work in bioethics can contribute to a secular defense of wilderness preservation grounded in the value of wilderness *qua* wilderness. Additionally, I want to propose that the debate over wilderness preservation is best described as a debate over what Sandel calls "Promethean aspirations": a debate over the extent to which it is ultimately good or bad for us, as humans, to attempt to assume control over nature, be it human nature (the concern of bioethics) or nonhuman nature (the concern of environmental ethics). Second, I will return to, and argue for, the idea—hinted at in Jana Thompson's critique of ecocentrism in chapter 3—that the value of wilderness *qua* wilderness can be understood as a kind of spiritual or religious value in that the value of wilderness's otherness is, in a sense, analogous to the value of a divine or sacred otherness. Finally, I will reflect on the extent to which either Sandel's secular reasons, or some type of spiritual or religious reason (based on a spiritual or religious conception of wilderness's value), can provide adequate opposition to the OFW.

This final chapter has five parts. The first draws a parallel between bioethics and environmental ethic and shows how the debate about wilderness can be understood as a debate about Promethean aspirations. The second presents Sandel's secular argument against an unrestrained attempt to remake nature, and his argument in favor of what he calls the giftedness of life. The third considers the extent to which Sandel's argument for giftedness can be applied to a defense of wilderness *qua* wilderness, and whether Sandel's secular arguments generate sufficient reason to oppose the OFW. I argue that his notion of the value of giftedness helps explain the undesirability of a significantly or entirely artificial world (something like world-X), but that the value of giftedness does not supersede the value created by a limited augmentation of wilderness per the dictates of the OFW. The fourth part explores how the value of wilderness's otherness is, in some ways, analogous to a religious or spiritual value. I conclude the chapter, and the book, by suggesting that one implication of (and perhaps motive for) a spiritual or religious valuation of wilderness is that it permits a sort of teleological suspension of strictly ethical considerations, such that any arguments against wilderness, even moral arguments like the OFW, may not be compelling.

BIOETHICS AND ENVIRONMENTAL ETHICS: A PARALLEL

In some measure, both environmental ethics and bioethics have an interest in considering the extent to which human beings should seek to influence and control aspects of nature that were previously beyond our influence and control. A bioethicist might talk about the right, the utility, or the permissibility of managing a pregnancy, designing a person, or interfering with the natural processes of human life; an environmental ethicist might talk about the right, the utility, or the permissibility of managing a species, or designing an ecosystem, or interfering with the natural processes of nonhuman life. In both fields there is a common concern with if, how, and why human beings should knowingly, and sometimes intentionally, augment a natural given.[1]

Eugene Hargrove notes that environmental ethics, like bioethics, frequently finds itself having to weigh the value of naturalness against the value of health and welfare. If genetically engineered hearts can extend and enhance life, why not engineer them? And if the artificial manipulation of ecosystems can result in enough food to end world hunger, why not manipulate them? The responses are complicated if one finds the naturalness of hearts or the wildness of the ecosystems to be ultimately valuable (Hargrove 1989, 157).

As mentioned in chapter 2, Hargrove endorses an environmental view called "therapeutic nihilism." Therapeutic nihilism maintains that, at present, the best way for us to help the earth is to leave it alone, given that in most scenarios we lack the understanding necessary for fruitful intervention. This is an accurate assessment given humanity's current knowledge and capability, yet I think Hargrove is correct to be pessimistic about the viability of therapeutic nihilism as a long-term environmental strategy. Rapid advances in science and technology will make it increasingly difficult to claim that we humans do not know enough for our interventions to be sources of help rather than harm. "While improvements in the ability to make ecological predictions since [Aldo] Leopold's time are not a revolutionary leap forward," writes Hargrove, "they are substantial and can be expected to translate into greatly improved expertise at the applied level in the near future." He continues:

> If these improvements continue, with or without a major breakthrough, therapeutic nihilism will almost certainly become indefensible as a mainstream preservationist position: As in medicine today, it will then become an approach that is relevant and useful only in cases in which an appropriate technical solution is not yet available. (Ibid., 161)

Writing in 1989, Hargrove seems to anticipate many ideas coming from the Breakthrough Institute. And if the coming indefensibility of therapeutic nihilism was detectable then, it is increasingly apparent today in the fields of medicine *and* ecology. Medical doctors still take a Hippocratic oath, and surely they still wish to "do no harm." But that traditional medical maxim now permits a dizzying array of procedures and treatments that would have shocked the Greek physician for whom it is named. As our medical knowledge and skill increases, so too will the set of actions that the maxim "do no harm" finds acceptable, even obligatory. Why not think that a similar trend exists within ecology and environmental science?

Realizing that the time of therapeutic nihilism may be coming to an end, Hargrove also anticipates the present inquiry. "The vulnerability of therapeutic nihilism to future developments in ecology puts environmentalists in an unusual and unpleasant situation. Either they must actively root against advances in ecology or look for better preservationist arguments" (ibid.). Some environmentalists seem attracted to the former option, railing against the science and rationality that ground modern ecology (See, for example, Gomez-Pompa and Kaus 1998 and Snyder 2008).[2] This book, by contrast, has attempted to do the latter.

Reckoning with Prometheus

A parallel between bioethics and environmental ethics is strengthened when we observe how participants in both conversations invoke the story of Prometheus. Recall that the full title of Mary Shelley's 1818 novel is: *Frankenstein; or, the Modern Prometheus*. According to one legend, the titan Prometheus gained infamy by stealing fire from the gods and sharing it with humans. For giving humans a power that was not rightly theirs—a power only the gods were fit to wield—Zeus punished Prometheus by chaining him to a rock in the Caucuses where, every day, an eagle arrived to eat his liver. Given Shelley's subtitle, a moral assessment of Dr. Frankenstein is in some part informed by a moral assessment of Prometheus. On the one hand, if Prometheus erred in seeking to give humanity control over that which it ought not control, then perhaps Frankenstein erred in a similar way. On the other hand, if Prometheus is a hero for transgressing arbitrary boundaries with the aim of benefiting mankind, perhaps Frankenstein deserves our admiration. It is fitting, then, to find both Bruno Latour and Michael Sandel directly invoking Prometheus.

Latour, as we have seen, tells us that Frankenstein, the modern Prometheus, did nothing wrong by trying to increase the power of man and improve his lot in life. These were heroic actions. Frankenstein's sin was a lack of courage and fortitude to see his project through. When Sandel invokes Prometheus, however, the message is very different. He acknowledges that genetic enhancement and genetic engineering are worrisome because they threaten to "undermine effort and erode human agency." But this is not the real problem. "The deeper danger," says Sandel, "is that they [genetic enhancement and genetic engineering] represent a kind of hyperagency, a Promethean aspiration to remake nature, including human nature, to serve our purposes and serve our desires" (Sandel 2007, 26–27).

If a Promethean aspiration to remake nature is worrisome for bioethics, it should be equally worrisome for environmental ethics. Bernard Williams drives the point home when he observes that our "restraint in the face of nature, a sense very basic to conservation concerns, will be grounded in a form of fear: a fear not just of the power of nature itself, but of what might be called Promethean fear" (Williams 1994, 51). We might fairly say that environmental ethics, like bioethics, is struggling with the question of whether to be or not to be Prometheus. If Sandel's anti-Promethean argument has merit, if there is value *for us* in taking some portion of human nature as it is rather than seeking to create or control it, then perhaps, *mutatis mutandis*, there is a similar argument to be made in defense of taking some portion of the nonhuman natural world as it is, rather than attempting to bring it under the umbrella of human control—in other words, an argument in defense of wilderness *qua* wilderness.

SANDEL ON MASTERY AND GIFTEDNESS

Sandel takes up the Promethean question by exploring a moral difficulty created by the human desire to master nature in the field of bioethics (Sandel 2007). He recognizes that advances in medical science and technology have the enormous potential to improve and extend human life. In some cases, he takes this new power to be a good thing.[3] But he also expresses profound concern over an unchecked drive toward a mastery and control of nature from which many of these advances emerge. Sandel is not worried about monsters; he is not afraid that a rogue Dr. Frankenstein will accidentally unleash malicious biological freaks. Nor is his enthusiasm for medical science inhibited by a theistic dogma in which we do wrong, in principle, by seeking to interfere with or usurp a divinely conceived system. At bottom, Sandel urges us to resist the drive toward mastery because doing so will make for better human lives.

Sandel's objection to unrestricted human enhancement and engineering (genetic or otherwise) is especially useful for our purposes because it seeks to uncover the essential wrongness of such endeavors and the essential value of giftedness. Typically, critics of human enhancement and engineering cite concerns that we might call coincidentally wrong, i.e., concerns that might themselves be ameliorated without the wrongness of genetic engineering and enhancement going away. The most common coincidental concerns are health and fairness. But for Sandel, concerns over health and fairness fail to get at the truly troublesome aspect of an attempt to control human nature. He uses athletics and the debate over performance enhancing drugs (PEDs) to illustrate the point.

Why, for example, might we think that athletes should not use PEDs? "The most familiar argument," writes Sandel, "is that they endanger athletes' health" (Sandel 2007, 35). This is true, but it does not get to the root of our unease with artificial enhancement. Imagine that steroids have been improved to the point that they are as harmless as multivitamins. Would we then approve of baseball players popping them between innings? Would we give them to little leaguers along with ice water and orange slices? That seems unlikely. Something bothers us about PEDs beyond their potential adverse effects on health.

Perhaps our real objection to PEDs is not that they endanger health, but that they are a form of cheating. After all, we think it is wrong for baseball players to cork their bats and put pine tar on their gloves, though neither practice carries a medical risk. But, like concerns over health, Sandel thinks cheating cannot be the root cause of our unease with enhancement. Suppose that Major League Baseball, excited by a new generation of medically safe PEDs, changes its rules to permit pharmaceutical enhancement. We could no longer object to steroids on the ground that they are a form of cheating if the new rules allow them. The commissioner could even ensure fairness by making the safe drugs equally available to all teams (ibid., 35–36). Would a simple rule change ameliorate our moral unease with PEDs? Again, probably not. Making PEDs legal would only solve the moral problem if we thought that rightness or goodness of an act is determined by the act's legality. But this gets things the wrong way round: we try to determine legality based on what we think is right or good.

For Sandel, the real trouble with PEDs (and other forms of enhancement) isn't that they threaten our health or violate a rule, but that they corrupt an essential aspect of sport "that celebrates natural talents and gifts" (ibid., 44). When we go to a baseball game, we are not looking to see how far a ball can be launched after contact with piece of wood. If we were, mechanized robotic performances would do just as well. Instead, we are looking to see what human nature can achieve when directed toward a certain end and willfully habituated in certain excellences.

Sandel grounds a fundamental objection to PEDs in his larger objection to the Promethean aspirations to remake nature. "The problem," he writes, "is not the drift toward mechanism but the drive to mastery. And what the drive to mastery misses, and may even destroy, is an appreciation of the gifted character of human powers and achievements" (ibid., 27).

The objection to PEDs is just one example of Sandel's larger objection to human enhancement and engineering. He thinks, however, that the line of reasoning that helps us to see what, at bottom, is wrong with PEDs in sports can help us to understand a fundamental concern with medical, pharmaceutical, and genetic enhancement of human beings in general. The fundamental concern centers on his notion of the giftedness of life.

The Value of Giftedness

A gift is something we receive rather than achieve; something we accept rather than choose.[4] To say that life has the quality of giftedness is to point out at least four things characteristic of human life: (a) we did not choose to be born; (b) we did not choose our genetic inheritance; (c) we initially have little control over our upbringing; and (d), as a result of (a), (b), and (c), much of who we are and what we can do is a matter of passive acceptance rather than active achievement.

Bioethics takes special interest in the human relation to (a) and (b). There is little an individual can do about (a) so far as it relates to one's self—we can end our life, but we cannot become unborn. Nevertheless, concerns over (a) affect us inasmuch as they affect the children we do or do not have or make, how we do or do not have or make them, and the reasons why; and (b) is significant for both extant and future individuals. The desire to exert more control over (a) and (b) is a kind of Promethean aspiration, a drive to mastery. The reason Sandel worries about the drive to mastery—genetic, pharmaceutical, and medical—is because it is in fundamental opposition to the giftedness of life.

The term "gift" has positive connotations. There are bad gifts (and bad gift givers), but a gift is generally a good thing—Sandel is telling us something about his assessment of the giftedness of life merely by using the term that he does. The question is: why does he see the giftedness of life as sufficiently good such that its preservation merits opposing forms of enhancement and engineering that would compromise it?

Sandel contends that all biological drives toward a mastery of human nature—from eugenics to PEDs—"represent a one-sided triumph of willfulness over giftedness, dominion over reverence, molding over beholding" (ibid., 85). Religious persons could condemn such a drive as a form of impiety, but "the moral stakes," he writes, "can also be described in secular terms," obviating the need to confront the metaphysical and epistemological challenges of theism. Even without invoking the divine, Sandel argues that the value of the giftedness of life can be seen when we envision how its elimination would "transform three key features of our moral landscape—humility, responsibility, and solidarity" (ibid., 86). Transformations can be good or bad, but as Sandel sees it this transformation would be for the worse. Humility and solidarity would be undermined, while responsibility would burgeon to oppressive proportions.

First, Sandel claims that the giftedness of life fosters humility, a virtue indispensable to moral maturity since it is precisely an "openness to the unbidden" involving an understanding that we are limited beings with limited control over our fates. Sandel singles out parenting as a kind of "school for humility." "That we care deeply for our children," he writes, "and yet cannot choose the kind we want, teaches parents to be open to the unbidden. Such openness is a disposition worth affirming" (ibid.). Even a benevolent, liberal eugenics program (one stripped of racism, coercion, and totalitarian aspirations) would create a situation in which parents affirm their design choices rather than learning to love the children they happen to have. And the possibility of postnatal genetic improvement would encourage an impulse to correct rather than adapt and accept.

Sandel also worries that bioengineering will increasingly make the idea of the self-made man a reality. Want to be taller? Stronger? More intelligent or empathetic? Better with numbers or more artistically inclined? The possibility of such "improvements" becomes increasingly likely as we continue to discover a genetic basis for many human physical, mental, and behavioral traits. Should this happen, "it would be difficult to view our talents as gifts for which we are indebted rather than achievements for which we are responsible" (ibid., 86–87). The danger here is that as our sense of humility decreases, the burden of our responsibility grows to immoderate proportions.

When we believe that we are in control, that we are responsible for who and what we are, "we attribute less to chance and more to choice." Parents may become (or may at least come to feel) directly responsible for their children's athletic, academic, artistic and moral failings, and individuals may start to assume responsibility for all their personal shortcomings. "One of the blessings of seeing ourselves as creatures of nature, or God, or fortune," says Sandel, "is that we are not wholly responsible for the way we are" (ibid., 87). The world and our human nature is, in large measure, a given. We do the best we can with what we have, and, like Epictetus, learn to accept what we cannot change. The drive to mastery undermines a Stoic approach to the world because it threatens to turn everything into a choice. Even individuals who opt out of genetic testing or genetic enhancement cannot opt out of the "burden of choice" such possibilities create. Choosing not to enhance or test oneself or one's child is still a choice. In such a world, we all become saddled with a new "moral burden" (ibid., 88).

In addition to an absence of humility and an increased burden of moral responsibility (genuine or merely presumed), Sandel believes that a rejection of the giftedness of life will trigger a decrease in social solidarity. Increased responsibility "for our own fate, and that of our children, may diminish our sense of solidarity with those less fortunate than ourselves" because the more we accept "the chanced nature of our lot, the more reason we have to share our fate with others" (ibid., 89). Consider the lesson of insurance. Since we do not know and cannot control when we will be affected by a medical or natural disaster, we pay into a common fund that protects us if the worst comes to pass. "Even without mutual obligation," notes Sandel, "people pool their risks and resources, and share one another's fate" (ibid., 89). But in a world where some people can select "good" genes, the enhanced would hesitate to share the risk of the unenhanced. And they may not feel guilty for doing so if enhancement is seen as a choice for which we bear personal, moral responsibility. Ultimately, Sandel fears that "genetic enhancement, if routinely practiced, would make it harder to foster the moral sentiments that social solidarity requires" (ibid., 90–91). Only a "lively sense of the contingency of our gifts," he writes, will prevent the "smug assumption that success is the crown of virtue" (ibid., 91).

Lastly, Sandel invokes the preservation of human freedom as a reason to value the giftedness of life. He borrows the curious idea from Jürgen Habermas. "[W]e experience our own freedom," says Habermas, "with reference to something which, by its very nature, is not at our disposal" (ibid., 81). Habermas means that thinking of ourselves as free requires looking back "to a beginning which eludes human disposal . . . something—like God or nature—that is not at the disposal of some *other* person" (ibid., 81–82). One of the reasons that Habermas, like Sandel, favors natural birth over the engineering of human beings is because birth, "being a natural fact, meets the conceptual requirement of constituting a beginning we cannot control" (ibid., 82).[5]

To summarize: Sandel believes that the giftedness of life is a valuable feature of our moral landscape. He further believes that a Promethean aspiration to remake nature—human nature, in this case—will damage this moral landscape in three ways. First, by reducing the sense of humility with which we regard ourselves and approach the world; second, by adding a moral burden to our existence by creating an explosion of responsibility; and third, by diminishing our sense of solidarity with our fellow humans, especially those less fortunate that ourselves, as a result of our decreased sense of humility and increased sense of responsibility. In addition, he draws on an idea from Habermas to suggest that the giftedness of life—a condition ensuring that we are not the product of human design and planning—may be necessary in order for us to experience ourselves as free beings. Finally, he maintains that his entire account of the value of giftedness and the danger of mastery can be defended on purely secular grounds.

GIFTEDNESS AND WILDERNESS

I will not pass judgment on Sandel's arguments against human enhancement and engineering. Doing so would take me too far afield from the topic of wilderness and would require a more thorough treatment of Sandel and his critics than what I've given here. My interest in Sandel is limited to a consideration of whether his reflections on the value of giftedness can support, or can begin to support, an argument in defense of wilderness *qua* wilderness, and whether an argument along these lines could be enough to oppose the OFW.

On the one hand, Sandel's appeal to the value of humility, solidarity, and responsibility make an important contribution to an understanding of the wilderness's value. The value of giftedness elaborated by Sandel does generate a significant reason to oppose an entirely, or even a maximally, artificial world.[6] On the other hand, I do not think that an appeal to this value amounts to a defense of wilderness *qua* wilderness, nor do I think it provides the resources to adequately rebuff the moral claims of the OFW.

Humility, Solidarity, Freedom, and Wilderness

Sandel's defense of giftedness initially seems promising for a defense of wilderness. Wilderness is the natural world retaining its primeval characteristics, insignificantly influenced by human activity—past or present, intentional or unintentional, conspicuous or inconspicuous. It is nature as given. We could say, then, that the preservation of wilderness is the preservation of the *giftedness* of the nonhuman natural world. If the giftedness of human nature is worth accepting and preserving, then perhaps the same is true of the giftedness of nonhuman nature. But Sandel's appeal to the value of humility, responsibility, solidarity, and the experience of human freedom are of limited use for a defense of wilderness *qua* wilderness.

Few contest that the experience of wilderness is humbling. Hikers living for days or weeks in the backcountry; fishermen battling storms and currents; even landscapers and contractors up against persistent gophers and serpentine root systems—to greater and lesser degrees, all come away with an appreciation of the power and unpredictability of wilderness and the challenges that accompany a foray into its domain. Such appreciation can foster a sense of humility, the recognition that, more often than not, it is we who must bend to the will of wild nature and not the other way around. But a defense of wilderness based on its value as a source of humility runs into a familiar problem. Wilderness is a sufficient condition for the habituation of a sense of humility, but it is not a necessary one. As Sandel reminds us, parenting is good source of humility; so is teaching, learning to rock climb, living in a foreign country, attempting to play ninety minutes of competitive soccer, and taking up the cello.

There is a second reason we cannot ground a defense of wilderness *qua* wilderness on the value of humility. Even if the nonhuman natural world is sufficiently altered such that it no longer makes sense to speak of any part of it as wilderness (though note that the OFW does not require such an extreme augmentation), there is no reason to think that the nonhuman natural world will lose the ability to humble us. Physicists, biologists, and engineers—all of whom look deeply into nonhuman nature and in many cases seek to intentionally manipulate and augment it—are often those who are *most* humbled by its power, its complexity, its mystery, and its beauty. Consider also the experience of high-altitude mountaineers. It is sometimes said that these climbers destroy the wilderness conditions of the mountains they climb simply by setting foot in places where humans had not yet tread. Even granting this dubious assertion,[7] it should be noted that truly great mountaineers become great by learning to humble themselves in and to the wilderness, by approaching their projects with a profound sense of humility before wild nature. Climbers occasionally talk about conquering mountains, but this is metaphor; big mountains are survived, not conquered. It is true that wilderness provides opportunities for the development of humility, but it is not a necessary condition for the virtue. It is also true that a sense of humility is actually a hallmark of individuals—be they scientists or adventurers—who intentionally intervene in wilderness and, by their agency, shape it.

The value of solidarity as the ground for a defense of wilderness does not fare any better than the value of humility. Even if wilderness is found to be a sufficient condition for a sense of social solidarity, it surely is not a necessary one: solidarity exists among citizens of New York, Amsterdam, and Beijing. More important, it is unclear in what sense wilderness can be said to foster solidarity, and whether the benefit of the solidarity it fosters is worth the cost.

Admittedly, all human beings are vulnerable to the variable dangers of wild nature. Even restricting ourselves to a consideration of natural disasters, it is clear that each of us is a potential victim of droughts, earthquakes, volcanoes, tsunamis, and hurricanes. In this sense, wild nature puts us all in the same boat. It is not uncommon to hear those affected by a natural disaster claim that the disaster brought people together in an inspiring way (neighbors helping neighbors, strangers helping strangers, aid pouring in from around the globe). Without denying the phenomenon of disaster-solidarity (and while realizing that it still only amounts to a sufficient condition), I think natural disasters in fact argue against wilderness.

The suffering caused by natural disasters is beyond measure. Enormous sums of time, energy, thought and money are spent trying to predict them and then mitigate their effects. If it somehow became possible (without instigating even worse ecological disasters) to prevent catastrophic earthquakes and volcanic eruptions, what would we say to a person who argues that we should not prevent them by interfering in the operation of wild nature because these disasters promote solidarity? The kindest thing we might say is that he is naïve, that he does not see that the cost outweighs the benefit. He would sound a bit like a person who, realizing the connection between World War II and the creation of the United Nations, and taking the existence of the United Nations to be a good thing, argues that the former was, in itself, a good thing because it hastened the arrival of the latter. The fact that some aspects of wilderness can, on occasion, promote solidarity is not enough to defend the preservation of these aspects, let alone wilderness *qua* wilderness.

Another of Sandel's reasons for valuing the giftedness of life rests on Habermas's suggestion that, in order to experience ourselves as free beings, we as individuals must have an origin not of our own making and not of the making of any other person. Our beginning as individuals must, in some sense, be seen as the work of "nature, or God, or chance," and not the result of human agency. But it is difficult to see how Habermas's suggestion can be turned into a defense of wilderness *qua* wilderness. Indeed, it is difficult to understand the meaning of the suggestion.

Part of the difficulty is due to the fact that Sandel invokes and quotes Habermas without presenting an argument, and without an argument, it is hard to respond positively or negatively. Assuming, however, that the preservation of a sense of freedom is a good reason to favor the natural birth of human infants over the designed creation of human beings, we must recognize that this idea applies explicitly to what Habermas and Sandel call natality: "the fact that human beings are born and not made" (ibid.). Perhaps it is the case that a human who is made cannot enjoy the same freedom as a human who is born—it is a complicated idea meriting further study. But the presence or absence of wilderness, even understanding it as the giftedness of the nonhuman natural world, lacks a clear connection to concerns over natality. Sandel appeals to Habermas in the course arguing for the value of the preservation of the giftedness of *human* nature. I see no reason why an intentional diminishing of the wilderness would necessarily jeopardize the giftedness of human nature. Babies can be (and are) born and not made in the non-wildernesses of New York, Amsterdam, and Beijing, and the natality of these babies is not conditional on the existence, somewhere else, of untrammeled land retaining its primeval characteristics.[8]

The final value of giftedness cited by Sandel concerns moral responsibility. I believe his concerns about an explosion of moral responsibility in the face of increased human mastery over nature are prescient and well founded. I further believe that these concerns illuminate an important anthropocentric reason to preserve the wilderness *qua* wilderness.

Responsibility and Wilderness

Sandel argues that a loss of the sense of the giftedness of life would unleash a torrent of moral responsibility. This worry has more purchase than his appeal to humility, solidarity, and freedom, at least so far as wilderness is concerned. To assume control is always to assume some measure of responsibility, and responsibility, particularly moral responsibility, is a weighty thing.

Consider the expanding circle of anthropocentric moral responsibility. Many of us have become increasingly attached to the idea that we all share some measure of moral responsibility for the well-being of all our fellow humans. We study, teach, and preach something called global justice; we are encouraged to be conscious of how our choice of food, clothing, language, and music affect those around us as well as people in faraway places; and we try to set aside nationalistic and racial fealties in favor of cosmopolitan humanism. For those attracted to this ideal, the burden of moral responsibility can be enormous. Seemingly every choice one makes can become fraught with moral confusion.[9]

Now imagine that you as an individual, or we as a species, also assume some responsibility for the welfare of nonhuman sentient life along the lines suggested by the OFW. The weight of our moral responsibility would increase massively. Wilderness, the ultimate given, would be transformed into a burdensome arena of choice—and not just choice, but *moral* choice.

Sojourns in the wilderness often act as what we might call moral holidays: time spent in a place where one is temporarily relieved of most of one's moral burdens. This is not to say that one acts, or would be permitted to act, *immorally* in the wilderness. Rather, the feeling of a moral holiday is a response to the fact that wilderness is an *a*moral sphere, and to the extent that we make ourselves a temporary part of the wilderness (perhaps even making the normative claim that we *ought* to make ourselves one with the wilderness), we can briefly live and act as but one more amoral part of amoral nature. Perhaps one maintains the moral belief that one morally ought to maintain the wilderness, but such a thought would only reinforce the idea that morality should be conspicuously absent in the wilderness. Taking on some responsibility for the welfare of wild creatures would severely lessen the anthropogenic enjoyment of what Jamieson describes as the wilderness's indifference. Rather than functioning as an escape from the moral burden of being human, the existence of wilderness would increase the burden significantly.

There is a connection between the value of wilderness as the value of a domain we neither create nor control and Sandel's worry about the moral burden of responsibility. If wilderness becomes anything other than such a domain, if it becomes an arena of moral choice, then the burden of responsibility creeps in. The anthropocentric value of not being—or of not feeling ourselves to be—morally responsible for wilderness and many of the creatures therein is a powerful reason to want to defend wilderness *qua* wilderness and to be wary of an increasingly human-managed, artificial world. Nevertheless, I do not find a concern about responsibility to be a sufficient moral reason to oppose the limited augmentation of the wilderness advocated by the OFW. At best, it could be a prudential reason for humanity to augment wilderness with caution and the awareness that, should humans seek to substantially intervene in the wilderness, we cannot panic and run away like Dr. Frankenstein when we start having second thoughts.

I reiterate that, at the present moment, our dealings with wilderness ought to be guided by some version of the precautionary principle or therapeutic nihilism: let us do no harm. But if and when it becomes probable that deliberate human intervention in the wilderness is likely to do more good than harm for morally considerable beings, it would be the height of moral cowardice to choose inaction on the grounds that moral responsibility is hard. Scientific and technological advances thus alter the parameters of the old Kantian insight: if we should, then we can; if we cannot, then we should not.

Introductory courses in ethics often present students with scenarios designed to probe their moral intuitions. A scenario familiar to most teachers of ethics asks students to imagine walking by a pond and seeing a person who appears to be drowning. What should we do and why? Invariably, one student responds with something like: *"You shouldn't try to help them because, if you do, you're implicated. It's all on you. You are responsible for what happens."* Gaps in the reasoning aside, the student's point is always clear: get involved, and you take on some moral responsibility for what happens; steer clear, and you avoid it. The hidden premise is that moral responsibility is hard and should, when possible, be avoided.

Responses of this kind push the class toward a discussion of moral responsibility. Can we really avoid it just by walking away? Even if we can, is the maxim 'avoid moral responsibility' something we want to endorse? Most students come around to the view that walking away does not necessarily absolve them of moral responsibility, and it would not be the right thing to do even if it did. Sometimes the class goes on to discuss the extent to which one can ever be obligated to assume a moral burden, and whether a moral argument can be rejected on the grounds that its prescription is too demanding, that the burden it creates is *too* heavy to reasonably be taken up. One outcome of the discussion is the simple but important insight that while moral responsibility can be hard, this isn't a sufficient reason to avoid it.

The same insight applies equally to the worry that, as we decrease a sense of the giftedness of life, we may increase the moral burden of responsibility we bear. Moral responsibility should not be assumed lightly, and a great deal of work needs to be done before we can understand what it would mean—ethically, ecologically, and phenomenologically—for humanity to augment wilderness along lines supported by the OFW (let alone what it would mean to become the intentional designers and managers of the biosphere and the inhabitants of a mostly artificial world). Nevertheless, my previous point holds: a desire to avoid, to minimize, or simply to diminish moral responsibility is, on its own, an insufficient reason to avoid what we otherwise have a strong moral reason to do.

Augmenting wilderness in an attempt to alleviate the suffering of millions of morally considerable beings would place a previously unknown burden of moral responsibility squarely on humanity's shoulders. Humans surely have an anthropocentric reason to avoid such a burden. But the benefit to humanity in avoiding this moral burden shrinks to insignificance when compared to the benefit provided to millions and millions of nonhuman morally considerable beings. The comparison is similar to one often made by opponents of factory farming. No matter how much pleasure one gets from eating chicken (or how pained one would be to never eat chicken again), this pleasure pales in comparison to the suffering experienced by the factory-farmed chicken one eats. Any anthropocentric good resulting from leaving a wilderness exactly as we find it will not outweigh the nonanthropocentrically bad outcomes of doing so; any anthropocentrically bad results that ensue from a human augmentation of wilderness per the dictates of the OFW will not outweigh the nonanthropocentric good.

WILDERNESS VALUE AS SPIRITUAL OR RELIGIOUS VALUE

In chapter 4, the reflections of Edward Abbey and Bill McKibben illustrated the idea that the value of wilderness *qua* wilderness is the value of a domain that is other-than-human. Abbey's epiphany is to realize that he doesn't love the desert in spite of its status as a nonhuman antipode to civilization, but because of it. The otherness was not *a* valuable trait; it was *the* valuable trait. Similarly, McKibben laments how the demise of wilderness turns the world itself into artifact, and, in doing so, devalues his experience of the natural world. These reflections on the value of wilderness have a clear spiritual or religious tone. Rudolph Otto's theological concept of the wholly Other would be at home in Abbey's essay on the desert, while Otto's description of the divine as a *mysterium tremendum* syncs with McKibben's valuation of nature (Otto 1958). This section argues that the value of wilderness *qua* wilderness can be felicitously understood as a kind of religious or spiritual value. The final section, "Spiritual Value and the OFW," considers one implication that such a religious or spiritual valuation has for debates about wilderness preservation.[10]

The Sacred and the Wild

McKibben expresses anxiety over a world increasing controlled by man *even though* he admits that this world is often sensorially and functionally indistinguishable from a more natural world. He confesses that merely knowing that we have, in many ways, assumed control of nature brings on feelings of loneliness because—and this is a crucial insight—it makes him think "there is nothing but us." Two aspects of this remark deserve notice. First, it would not be uttered by a conventional theist; a conventional theist would be confused by the idea that an awareness of human agency in nature meant there is "nothing but us." Second, in claiming that the end of nature engenders feelings of loneliness, the belief that we humans are now all there is, and that the world is less meaningful as a result, McKibben is signaling that wilderness can be a substitute for God inasmuch as the nature and value of wilderness takes on the semblance of a nature and value most commonly associated with the sacred, the divine, or the religious (Recall that what McKibben calls "nature" is equivalent to what I am calling "wilderness").

McKibben's analogous understanding of wilderness and God, and environmentalism and faith, is evident in other remarks. He makes the somewhat awkward suggestion that the holocaust and the end of nature are similar in that both destroy faith and leave man feeling alone (McKibben 1990, 79). He argues for the natural over the artificial by saying that God cannot speak to us through Astroturf as he can through grass (ibid., 80). He also quotes naturalist John Burroughs, who, writing at the turn of the twentieth century, says "We now use the word Nature very much as our fathers used the word God . . . and, I suppose, back of it all we mean the power that is everywhere present and active, and in whose lap the visible universe is held and nourished" (ibid., 72).

An interpretation of wilderness's otherness as sacred is not unique to McKibben. Forrest Clingerman, for example, sees the otherness of wilderness as "Divine Otherness." "By instantiating the otherness of the Other," writes Clingerman, "wildness—as a critical border concept—is a place where philosophy and theology intersect." He goes on to argue that both philosophy and theology should converge "in the recognition that wild nature is the place where the world overflows beyond human control—nature as otherness transcends itself to offer the divine Other" (Clingerman 2010, 224). Scott Friskics compares wilderness to the Sabbath. "Like the Sabbath, wilderness invites us to suspend our commercial pursuits, relinquish our claims to ownership and control, and turn our attention toward the other-than-human ground of our being." He adds: "The ultimate significance of Sabbath observance and wilderness practice is that they may teach us to dwell . . . in holiness" (Friskics 2008. 398). Sigurd Olson, former director of the National Park Service, told Congress that "the spiritual values of wilderness" are "the real reason for all the practical things we must do to save wilderness" (Nagle 2005, 978). And in line with McKibben's existential lament, Physicist A. J. Rush reports: "When man obliterates wilderness" we will find that "in a deeply terrifying sense, man is on his own" (Nash 1967, 256).

The connection between the value of wilderness and the value of some sort of transcendent, other-than-human domain is further evidenced in the legislative debates over the 1964 Wilderness Act. John Nagle argues that proponents of the Act employed four distinct religious and spiritual reasons to support their cause: (1) wilderness preserves land as it was created by God; (2) wilderness is a place to encounter the divine; (3) wilderness is a venue for spiritual renewal; and (4) experiencing God's works in wilderness is an escape from the human. Hubert Humphrey was the initial sponsor of the legislation, and in promoting it he "asked his colleagues to consider the spiritual well-being of Americans." Senator Clinton Anderson endorsed the Act, saying: "Wilderness is a demonstration by our people that we can put aside a portion of this which we have as a tribute to the Maker and say—this we will leave as we found it" (Nagle 2005, 979).

Witness testimony from the congressional hearing is equally replete with references to the sacred value of the wilderness. Surprising some listeners, one oil executive proclaimed "the reservation of such wilderness areas" is "essential to the spiritual well-being of millions of Americans" (ibid., 980). A Denver resident confessed he had "never felt as close to god at any time or any place as in the wilderness" (ibid., 983). Another witness rebuffed the potential criticism that not many people actually visit the wilderness: "To argue that few visit wilderness is fallacious, because even those who might drive to its edge feel a spiritual uplift as they look off into an area where there is no pronounced desecration" (ibid., 980). One opponent of the legislation made it especially clear that wilderness advocates were valuing wilderness specifically as some other-than-human sacred realm, saying they "seem to regard the wilderness system as something special, something different . . . a holy of holies, as it were" (ibid., 986). This opponent was correct.

Several scholars have identified a strong connection between environmentalism and religiosity. Thomas Dunlap argues that environmentalism is a secular faith, and that the American environmental movement has been, in many ways, indistinguishable from an evangelical religious movement (Dunlap 2004, 2006). Scott Aiken makes the case that traditional and contemporary environmentalism tends to ground its normative claims in what he calls the "dogma of environmental revelationism," an epistemological position whose closest relative is a kind of religious dogma grounded in ecstatic, mystical experiences of the sacred that cannot be falsified (Aiken 2008). Aiken and Dunlap would agree with Mark Sagoff's assertion that environmentalism easily meets the criteria that "William James argued were necessary for a belief system to be a religion. . . . James wrote that a religious belief expresses a conviction that 'there is an unseen order, and that our supreme good lies in adjusting ourselves thereto'" (Sagoff 2015, 1).

The point I want to make is that there is a connection between wilderness essentially existing as a realm of the other-than-human, a domain of the world that we neither create not control, and the fact that, for many people, the value of wilderness assumes an aspect of sacred, spiritual, or religious value.[11] The Holy of Holies belongs to Judaism, but many religious traditions possess an equivalent: a temple, an inner sanctum, a shrine—some place where humans ought not go or some thing they ought not touch on the understanding that doing so would sully the sacred space or object, and would bridge a valuable gap that exists between profane humanity and some sacred, Holy and wholly Other. As the opponent of the Wilderness Act quoted above aptly observed, wilderness, as a domain of the other-than-human, seems capable of functioning as a Holy of Holies and fulfilling whatever profound spiritual desire such a place fulfills.

To be sure, wilderness is a worldly and natural other (not otherworldly or supernatural). But experience of the worldly otherness of wilderness generates, for some, the same kind of existential succor and spiritual satisfaction as experience of a supernatural other. In both cases, what appears to be valuable to many individuals is the maintenance of a cognitive or experiential connection to that which is radically not human, that which is in some sense a greater than humans, and, above all, that which humans did not create, should not control, and under whose partial dominion humans ought to remain.

Laurel Kearns of Drew Theological Seminary provides further evidence of the ability of the value of wilderness *qua* wilderness to substitute for traditional spirituality, noting, "the more biblically oriented one is, the less one is concerned about the environment." Comparing the congressional scorecard of members of the League of Conservation Voters with that of the Christian Coalition, she finds:

The first is the reverse mirror image of the second; politicians at the top of one list appear almost without exception on the bottom of the other. The idea that nature represents creation and is thus sacred plays much better to those whose religious views are secular than to those who views are grounded in church-based religion or in scripture. (Ibid., 3)

If we begin to understand the value of a domain that is neither human-created nor human-controlled as being analogous, in some respects, to the value of the existence of a sacred other, we can make sense of Kearns's finding. We can also make sense of McKibben's existential despair. There is comfort in believing that we are not "all there is," whether the something else is the Hebrew God, the Buddhist Dharma, or nonhuman Nature.

Sandel and Sanctity

Sandel repeatedly maintains that his valuation of giftedness is secular and that it need not be couched in religious terms (Sandel 2007, 86, 92–97). But Sandel himself gives cause to question the accuracy of his assessment. Despite his intent, Sandel's defense of giftedness invites a spiritual or religious reading and lends support to the idea that the value of wilderness—as the giftedness of the nonhuman natural world—can be understood as analogous to a religious or spiritual value.

To start, some of Sandel's language is conspicuously religious. In valuing the giftedness of life, he encourages us to adopt a stance of "openness to the unbidden," a phrase borrowed from theologian William F. May (former president of the American Academy of Religion and the Society of Christian Ethics). Consider also that Sandel describes the wrongness of eugenics as representing, *inter alia*, "the one-sided triumph of . . . dominion over reverence" (ibid., 85). Reverence can simply mean a show of deep respect, but the term's most common (nearly exclusive) application concerns some dimension of the sacred. Additionally, Sandel twice points out that it is better for children to owe their genetic inheritance to God, or nature, or chance than to a deliberate choice made by their parents. In saying this, Sandel seems to be using God as a placeholder for the unknown, perhaps for the unknowable. But this is not very different from how God is understood by many religious and spiritual persons, in many religious and spiritual traditions.

Sandel acknowledges the religious overtones of his paean to giftedness will lead some to conclude that his argument is not, as he claims, defensible in secular terms. For instance, one might assume "that to speak of a gift presupposes a giver. If this is true," notes Sandel, "then my case against genetic engineering and enhancement is inescapably religious." But he goes on to say that "an appreciation for the giftedness of life can arise from religious or secular sources," noting that it is commonplace to speak about a musician's gift or an athlete's gift without taking a stand on theism. "What we mean," says Sandel, "is simply that the talent in question is not wholly of the athlete's or musician's own doing." The gift might originate from God, but it might originate from nature or chance or some other force "that exceeds his control" (ibid., 92–93).

Similarly, Sandel admits that we often speak of nature and life as sacred but maintains that speaking of them this way does not commit us to some "metaphysical version of the idea" of sanctity (ibid.). What then does it commit us to? He gives several possibilities:

> For example, some hold with the ancients that nature is sacred in the sense of being enchanted, or inscribed with inherent meaning, or animated by divine purpose; others . . . view the sanctity of nature as deriving from God's creation of the universe; and still others believe that nature is sacred simply in the sense that it is not a mere object at our disposal, open to any use we may desire. (Ibid., 93–94)

Sandel is very close to contradicting himself. If the sanctity of nature is a result of its being enchanted or animated with divine purpose, then the sanctity *is* inescapably spiritual or religious. The same is true if the sanctity of nature is thought to derive from "God's creation of the universe." Sandel is left with two possible options for his nonreligious, nonspiritual interpretation of sanctity: sanctity as the possession of inherent meaning, and sanctity as the quality of not being a mere object.

What we find is that Sandel is essentially making an appeal for an understanding of sanctity as intrinsic value$_2$ (moral considerability). "These various understanding of the sacred," he writes, "all insist that we value nature and the living beings within it as more than mere instruments. . . . This moral mandate need not rest on a single religious or metaphysical background (ibid., 94). It is true that moral considerability does not rest on a single religious or metaphysical background. I affirm, with Sandel, that human life is sacred, understood here as morally considerable. But if, as his remarks indicate, Sandel wishes to justify an ascription of sanctity to nature itself, he will be stymied by the objections against any such ascription detailed in chapters 3 and 4.[12]

SPIRITUAL VALUE AND THE OFW

In "Giftedness and Wilderness" I argued that Sandel's secular defense of the value of giftedness contributes to an anthropocentric valuation of wilderness, and it provides a reason to be dubious about the prospect of a world increasingly under human management. But I also argued that a secular, anthropocentric valuation of a worldly domain that significantly retains the conditions of wilderness, and the desire to maintain a realm of giftedness for which we bear only a minimal responsibility of nonmaleficence, do not supersede the moral reason to make a limited augmentation of the wilderness as proposed in the OFW.

In "Wilderness Value as a Religious or Spiritual Value," I argued that we have ample reason to consider the value of wilderness *qua* wilderness to be analogous to a spiritual or religious value. Even Sandel was eager to justify an ascription of sanctity to nature or wilderness, though his account is remarkable for the fact it attempts to do so without acknowledging a metaphysical, theological, or spiritual grounding. He tries to use the language of secular liberal morality to justify a nontheistic ascription of sanctity as moral considerability, but if the sanctity in question is the sanctity of the wilderness—the moral considerability of the giftedness of the nonhuman natural world—the arguments against intrinsic value$_2$ that were elaborated in chapters 3 and 4 present decisive opposition. Sandel's secular appeal to sanctity is no more useful as an objection to the OFW, or as a defense of wilderness *qua* wilderness, than an appeal to humility, solidarity, and responsibility just considered in chapter 5.

I conclude this study by suggesting that an unabashedly religious or spiritual valuation of wilderness *qua* wilderness—a belief that wilderness *is* sacred in some theological or metaphysical sense—provides grounds for a nonethical opposition to the OFW. It provides grounds *not* because such a valuation generates a moral reason to preserve wilderness that is stronger than the moral reason to augment it generated by the OFW, but because, as a type of spiritual or religious valuation, it may be thought to supersede the ethical prescription of the OFW. That being said, a religious or spiritual valuation of wilderness generates a distinct set of philosophical, moral, and political dangers that ought not be ignored. Moreover, even if a difference between religious and moral grounds is countenanced, it remains debatable whether a defense of wilderness preservation grounded in a religious valuation of wilderness is sufficient to withstand the moral reasons generated by OFW to oppose such preservation.

From the Ethical to the Religious

If wilderness is valued *qua* domain of the other-than-human, as a sort of natural Holy of Holies, or wholly Other, or *mysterium tremendum*, then moral arguments such as those generated by the OFW may not be as compelling as they would be when grounded in a strictly secular valuation of wilderness.

Religious reasons and religious justification are often thought to be distinct from, and untranslatable into, secular moral reasons. The most powerful expression of this idea is still Kierkegaard's distinction between ethical and religious stages of thinking, and his argument that the religious stage may involve a nonrational teleological suspension of the ethical.

Kierkegaard introduces the teleological suspension of the ethical in conjunction with the story of Abraham and Isaac. He argues that the teleological suspension of the ethical is necessary if we are to understand Abraham as anything other than a madman or a murderer. We may ultimately decide that Abraham *was* unstable or immoral, but if we do then we must relinquish all talk of faith and concede that religion is, at best, just what Hegel thought it was: *Vorstellung*, picture-thinking, a necessary but lower order of reason.[13] If we wish to maintain the belief that Abraham's act was one of faith rather than madness, and that faith might permit or require acts that cannot be translated into a rationally ethical idiom, then we must be open to the idea of the religious as distinct from the ethical. We must also accept that religious claims may be capable of superseding ethical claims, not because they contradict or disprove the ethical claims, but because the ethical claims undergo a teleological suspension that cannot itself be explained or defended in ethical terms.

In the story, God commands Abraham to sacrifice his son Isaac. Abraham complies and journeys with Isaac to Mt. Moriah where he prepares an altar and binds the boy. At the last moment, God intervenes and Isaac is spared. The story is usually interpreted as a test of Abraham's devotion. As such, Abraham is great because he is willing to give up that which he loves most, and God is great because he does not actually require the sacrifice.

Kierkegaard suggests that this interpretation fails to grasp the true nature of Abraham's act because it remains within the sphere of the rational and the ethical. It allows us to understand Abraham as a tragic hero, but not the father of faith. A tragic hero is one who overcomes, through suffering and sacrifice, his particularity (his particular desires, loves, joys, and interest) in favor of that which he takes to be a higher, universal demand. The overcoming of the particular in favor of the universal is what Kierkegaard calls the ethical. The ethical is both rational and communicable. Agamemnon became a tragic hero when he sacrificed his daughter Iphigenia to ensure the Greeks a favorable wind and the chance to sail for Troy. He overcame his particular feelings of love and paternal obligation and forced himself to give up one thing in order to gain another. Agamemnon may have been wrong to act as he did, but we understand the act and can evaluate it with the use of moral reason.

In the language of contemporary political philosophy, we might say that, for Kierkegaard, the movement from the ethical to the religious involves a movement beyond public reason: a movement beyond "forms of reasoning and argument available to citizens generally."[14] We might disagree with Agamemnon, but his moral reasoning is understandable in a way that Abraham's is not. To move from the ethical to the religious is to move beyond a realm of publicly accessible reason.

Kierkegaard denies that Abraham was like Agamemnon. To be sure, Abraham could still have been great had he been a tragic hero: to sacrifice the particular (his love for his son) in favor the universal (God's will) could potentially have been a noble thing. Yet Kierkegaard argues that Abraham was not a tragic hero but a knight of faith. Abraham is willing to sacrifice his only son, but as a knight of faith he trusts in God's earlier promise that he will leave countless descendants and father a great nation. He believes even though his rationality scoffs at such belief. How can an old man kill his only son and still expect countless descendants? Reason cannot make sense of this belief, nor justify it in a way that is publicly accessible, because it isn't a rational belief.

The knight of faith believes by virtue of the absurd. This kind of belief marks an Abraham off from an Agamemnon, and marks what Kierkegaard sees as true religious conviction off from disguised secular rationality. After all, Agamemnon is also supposed to have been acting on religious principles—the goddess Diana demanded a sacrifice. But notice how different Agamemnon's religious conviction is from Abraham's. Agamemnon did not expect to give up the particular in favor of the universal and still somehow retain the particular. He knew that killing his daughter meant killing his daughter, giving her up for a greater good. He understood this fact and expected his fellow Greeks to understand it as well. Kierkegaard draws attention to the fact that Abraham does not resign himself to losing his son. Through faith, by virtue of the absurd and a belief that flies in the face of reason, he expects to give up Isaac and yet still have him. He trusts that God has a plan even if he fails to understand it; in other words, he places his trust in another person not in a rational principle. Abraham does not believe that his reason for action is, in principle, intelligible to all rational beings, nor does he think that it is based on premises he can reasonably expect others to accept. His action requires a leap of faith, a term Kierkegaard's coins to describe (if not explain) Abraham's behavior.[15]

CONCLUSION: FROM WILDERNESS ETHICS TO WILDERNESS FAITH?

Without endorsing one normative theory over any other, I couched the OFW in consequentialist, utilitarian terms because it makes the case for the moral considerability of some nonhuman animals less controversial than an approach grounded in deontology or virtue ethics. Expressing the OFW in consequentialist, utilitarian terms is sufficient to generate a *pro tanto* reason to favor human augmentation of the wilderness, which, after all, is all the OFW attempts to do. But notice that moral reasoning of the OFW loses force if wilderness is valued in religious or spiritual rather than moral terms.

The value of a sacred place, a Holy of Holies, is not cashed out in utilitarian calculations. For the spiritual and religious, such a place just *is* valuable and simply *ought* to exist. It would even seem profane to try and explain how a place, designated as a Holy of Holies, is only valuable because it helps or harms something. An appeal to the inviolable value of the existence of wilderness is a kind of appeal to nonanthropocentric intrinsic value. Chapter 3 and chapter 4 argued that an ascription of nonanthropocentric intrinsic value to wilderness is not reasonable in any sense.[16] But if—believing wilderness to be sacred, a divine wholly Other—one has moved from the ethical to the religious, then moral reasons may not be compelling. In fact, one might concede that a rational, moral valuation of wilderness does argue in favor human intervention, yet still think that a spiritual valuation demands forbearance. The moral reasoning of the OFW would not be defeated, though it may, perhaps, be temporarily suspended.

Perhaps the desire of some environmentalists to reinvigorate an enchanted, spiritual view of the natural world, and their propensity to adopt dogmatic revelation-based epistemology, is linked to the idea that a domain functioning as a Holy of Holies would, in principle, be inviolable. And not just inviolable in the face of narrowly construed economic or hedonistic reasons—it would even be inviolable in the face of *moral* reasons. Dunlap, for instance, reports that some ecoterrorists (individuals who seek to terrorize and even kill perceived enemies of nature) justify their violence by pointing to the sacredness of that which they defend. This brand of *apologia* is a grim hallmark of religious terrorism (Dunlap 2004, 85).[17]

Charles Windsor, Prince of Wales and ardent environmentalist, goes so far as to claim that "only a sense of the sacred in dealing with the natural world" will lead to proper valuation of nonhuman nature and sustainable development. The "timelessness of traditional religion" must be brought to bear on environmental thinking, he says, because "It is the heart that experiences God, not the reason."[18] The implication of Windsor's remarks is that reason and "scientific rationalism" might keep us from valuing the wilderness as a sacred thing, and only a sacred valuation will preserve the wilderness from further human augmentation. For better or worse, he may be right (Windsor 2000).

But in a way this is my point. I have argued that rational, secular morality provides no inviolable defense for wilderness *qua* wilderness, and no reasonable opposition to a limited augmentation of the wilderness along the dictates of the OFW. Heterodox environmentalists, such as those from the Breakthrough Institute, may not find this troubling, but I suspect the orthodox will. If I am correct, it may be that the preservation of wilderness *qua* wilderness will require a sort of spiritual or religious ascription of sanctity—only such an ascription will ground a defense of wilderness in the kind of inviolable, intrinsic, absolute value capable of withstanding even a moral argument like the OFW. Nelson notes a potential political advantage in ascribing some sort of religious value to wilderness, at least in America. If "designated wilderness areas can be said to serve a religious function," they might come under the protection of the First Amendment, and could be defended on "grounds of freedom to worship as one chooses" (Nelson 1998, 169). Yet there would be a simultaneous political disadvantage.

A religious valuation of wilderness, and a religious defense of wilderness areas, is problematic for any society subscribing to a Rawlsian ideal of public reason in which citizens not only owe each other reasons for their political convictions, but reasons based on premises they can reasonably expect their fellow citizens to accept (see endnote 14 for an elaboration of the idea of public reason). As discussed, religious justification is often a paradigmatic example of the deployment of reasons that are explicitly and unapologetically *not* public. It may be that a religious defense of wilderness proves politically expedient, particularly in America, but a liberal democratic society should seriously question the desirability of grounding an ultimate defense of wilderness *qua* wilderness in spiritual or religious value.

Another potential difficulty to a defense of wilderness grounded a spiritual or religious value concerns the extent to which we are comfortable extending moral or legal exceptions on the basis of religious conviction. An ascription of religious value might lead to something like a teleological suspension of ethical such that the moral claims of the OFW are surmountable, if not refutable. This would be a dangerous strategy to employ, however, as it could open the door to the religious justification of acts and beliefs that are best left unjustified. Let us remember that Kierkegaard introduces the teleological suspension of the ethical in conjunction with attempted filicide.

It is not uncommon for otherwise impermissible or intolerable acts and beliefs to be permitted or tolerated so long as they derive from, or have significant attachment to, a religious conviction. A boss or a teacher is unlikely to give an employee or a student the day off to watch the World Cup, no matter how personally valuable or meaningful the student or employee claims the experience of watching soccer would be. But the same boss or teacher may be willing—even obligated—to give the same student or employee the day off in order to observe a religious holiday. In *Why Tolerate Religion?* Brian Leiter highlights public school policies that allow a Sikh boy to wear his kirpan (a religious ceremonial dagger) to school, while simultaneously prohibiting a different boy at that same school from wearing a treasured family knife that does not serve a religious function (Leiter 2013, 1–4). An exception is made for the religious boy and the religious knife, but not for secular boy and secular knife, even supposing the latter to be of immense personal value to the boy and his family. For better or worse, moral and legal exceptions are often made for religions and the religious specifically because they *are* religions and religious.[19]

The ethical stakes involved in allowing a student to miss class for a religious holiday but not to watch soccer, or to carry a ceremonial religious dagger but not a special hunting knife, are rather low. A society wishing to preserve religious freedom by maintaining a firm separation of church and state may feel that some moral and legal exceptions ought to be made for religion such that no citizen can reasonably claim state interference in his or her private religious life. The civic utility of such exceptions may be considered valuable enough that individual instances of unfair, preferential treatment toward religion will be tolerated.[20] Still, most agree that there are definite limits to the kind of exceptions that ought to be made.

One such generally accepted limitation concerns tolerance of that which clearly and grossly violates the welfare of a third party (ibid., 22). I cannot perform human sacrifice and expect a moral and legal exceptions to be made on the grounds that I am acting as a sincere follower of Tlaloc, an Aztec god who demands human blood, even supposing I *am* a sincere follower of Tlaloc. To take a less outlandish example, it remains morally and legally controversial whether devout Christian Scientists should be permitted, on the basis of sincere religious conviction, to withhold secular medical care from their children. The controversy arises from the fact that parents do not have an obvious right to harm, or even to withhold care from, their children in service of a religious principle.[21] So while some moral and legal exemptions for religion may be tolerable, it is at least controversial whether we ought to extend toleration to beliefs and practices that are clearly inimical to the welfare of other morally considerable beings.

If one believes that the religious principles of one set of morally considerable beings should not be tolerated once they become inimical to the basic welfare of some other set morally considerable beings, it becomes harder to see how an ascription of religious or spiritual value to wilderness could justify wilderness preservation. Anyone who registers moral unease when a religious conviction is used to justify failing to seek medical care for a sick child (when beneficial medical care is available) must also register moral unease when a religious conviction is used to justify the maintenance of a state of affairs predicated on suffering and early death (i.e., wilderness preservation) if and when there exists the possibility for beneficial human intervention. Assuming neither case involves malevolence—that is, assuming neither case involves the motivation to harm—the moral unease comes from the apparent prioritization of a personal religious conviction over the basic welfare of some other morally considerable being.[22]

Perhaps the value of wilderness *qua* wilderness is best understood as a kind of religious or spiritual value. Perhaps that which is of religious or spiritual value occasionally deserves moral and legal exemptions. But it is chilling to suggest that some other being must suffer in service to our religious values. Accordingly, a religious or spiritual turn in the defense of wilderness preservation should only be undertaken with full awareness of the accompanying philosophical, moral, and political perils.

NOTES

1. The connection is perhaps not surprising when we think that biology (the primary science of bioethics) and ecology (the primary science of environmental ethics) are related and overlapping.

2. Or consider the remarks of the royal environmental activist Charles Windsor, Prince of Wales. He states that the sacred trust between mankind and creator has been "smothered" by "scientific rationalism," and our only chance of avoiding environmental collapse is to stop "treating the world as a laboratory of life" and to recover a sense of nature as inviolable *because* it is sacred (Windsor 2000).

3. Sandel generally approves of genetic enhancement and engineering when it seeks to restore us to a natural condition of health; he opposes it when it seeks to make us "better than well." As my present interest in Sandel extends only so far as his ideas are relevant to the wilderness debate, I will not give a full treatment of his position on bioethics. I note, however, that Sandel's case is dependent on a robust conception of nature and the natural that he does not explain or defend.

4. Part of what can make cash or a gift card an awkward (though not unappreciated) gift is that it lacks these qualities. Such offerings ask the recipient to choose rather than accept, to actively acquire rather than passively receive. I suspect some of the awkwardness comes from the fact that we all intuitively realize there is something odd in receiving a gift that doesn't operate as a gift.

5. Nelson records an argument called "the salvation of freedom argument" but it is something quite different from what Sandel and Habermas seem to have in mind. Nelson points to the fact that the existence of large tracts of unpopulated or lightly populated land have, historically, acted as sanctuaries for those facing political tyranny. Some, like Edward Abbey, see a connection between political repression and increases in urbanization on the one hand (e.g., twentieth-century central Europe), and a connection between rural environments and revolutionary struggles on the other (e.g., Cuba and Vietnam in the twentieth century, and America in the late eighteenth century) (Nelson 1998, 181–82). A connection between freedom and wilderness also plays itself out in myth and literature. Robin Hood evaded political tyranny by hiding in Sherwood Forest; the savage in *Brave New World* craved the liberation

from social control that he previously enjoyed on his wilderness reservation. The salvation of freedom argument, like the other arguments in Nelson's amalgamation, is not an argument for wilderness *qua* wilderness. It is an argument for the wilderness as a place sometimes instrumentally useful for avoiding or combatting political tyranny.

6. Sandel's ethic of giftedness faces stiff opposition. Arguably the best reasons against a position like Sandel's can be found in Julian Savulescu's widely read article "Genetic Enhancement and the Ethics of Enhancement of Human Beings" (Savulescu 2007). Sandel makes it clear that he is responding to Savulescu's arguments (and others like it) in *The Case Against Perfection*.

7. See "Responses to the Emperical Objection," chapter 1, for an explanation of how wilderness is a condition that obtains by degree. Edmund Hillary and Tenzing Norgay did not destroy Everest as a wilderness by standing on the summit in 1953—though hordes of mountaineers *have* significantly diminished the wildness of Nepal's Khumbu region in the decades since.

8. Sandel's invocation of Habermas's concern about freedom to oppose the designing of human beings is puzzling. I have not provided cogent explanation of the idea because I am not sure what it would look like. But thinkers with the stature of Sandel and Habermas surely deserve a charitable reading, so let us grant that there may indeed exist an important connection between human freedom and natality in the realm of bioethics which awaits explication. The point I stress here is that such a concession still does not make the case for wilderness as a necessary condition for the experience of human freedom. However inspired Sandel's application of Habermas may turn out to be for bioethics, I maintain that it will be ineffective as an argument for the preservation of wilderness *qua* wilderness.

9. I lived near a café in Cambridge, Massachusetts, called the Clear Conscience Café. Having ethically sourced their products and justly compensated their staff (supposedly), their pitch to customers was that one could finally sit and enjoy a cup of coffee without feeling guilty. The café was popular. One wonders if the popularity was indicative of the moral guilt besetting many Cantabridgians.

10. Nelson identifies something called the "the cathedral argument" in his amalgamation of arguments in defense of wilderness preservation. The cathedral argument claims that wilderness functions, for some, as a "site for spiritual, mystical, or religious encounters." Muir said wilderness is a "window opening into heaven, a mirror reflecting the creator" (Nelson 1998, 186). It is worth noting that the cathedral argument usually relies on an understanding of the wilderness as God's unspoiled handiwork, from which a normative claim is derived that God's handiwork ought to remain unspoiled. I am suggesting that the spiritual or religious value of wilderness can also derive from the wilderness' status as a domain of the other-than-human, in which case the a spiritual or religious valuation of wilderness would be based on the value of wilderness *qua* wilderness. As the name of the cathedral argument indicates, wilderness is not the only place to have religious or spiritual encounter. It is, however, the only place to encounter a domain of a worldly other-than-human.

11. In "That Good Old-Time Wilderness Religion," J. Baird Callicott suggests that Holmes Rolston III's staunch defense of the received (traditional) wilderness idea and advocacy for traditional wilderness preservation is a product of, or at least

informed by, Rolston's religious orthodoxy (Presbyterian in Rolston's case). Callicott strongly implies that all defense of traditional wilderness—idea and place—may be dogmatically reliant on some form of religiosity. Callicott further speculates, on the basis of anecdotal evidence, that attachment to the traditional wilderness idea has a nontrivial correlation to Protestantism. He notes, for example, that the wilderness idea has been highly influential in the intellectual environmental history of Protestant Anglo-America and Australia, while playing "no significant role" in Catholic Latin America (Callicott 1998b, 388–99).

12. Sandel's use of the term "inherent meaning" suggests he might be appealing to intrinsic value$_3$ (inherent, non-relational value). But an attempt to justify the sanctity of wilderness won't fare any better even if we adopt this interpretation, given the strength of the arguments against ascribing intrinsic value$_3$ to wilderness presented in chapter 3.

13. This way of glossing Hegel's position is, to be sure, a bit of a caricature, given the systematic centrality that he attaches to religion, past and present. For Hegel, without religion there is no philosophy, even though philosophy ultimately supersedes it.

14. John Rawls explains the idea of public reason and what it means for a reason to be publicly accessible in a variety of ways. In *Political Liberalism*, public reasons are reliant on "forms of reasoning and argument available to citizens generally, and so in terms of common sense, and by the procedures and conclusions of science when not controversial." Public reason asks us to "live politically with others in the light of reasons all might reasonably be expected to endorse," and to consider what it is "reasonable to expect others to think who stand to lose when our reasoning prevails." To be considered public, "arguments and evidence supporting political judgments should, if possible, be not only sound but such that they can be publicly seen to be sound" (Rawls 1993, 162, 241). In "The Idea of Public Reason Revisited," Rawls writes that the standard of public reason requires that our public deliberation employ "premises we accept and think others could reasonably accept" (Rawls 1997, 786).

15. The leap, Kierkegaard notes, is akin to that of the ballet dancer's leap that succeeds not simply by leaving the ground but by coming back to the ground gracefully, as though she had never left it. In this regard her leap differs from someone who is following a script, a guideline, or general principle regarding how to leap. Abraham is a knight of faith because his relation to the divine is a relation to a person, not to a principle or idea (ethical or otherwise), and because that relation enters seamlessly into his existence, canceling the difference—as only love can—between two persons, even if one is divine. This emphasis on the religious value as interpersonal explains the metaphor of the ballet dancer's leap as something that requires the practice of loving concretely and creatively, superseding mere rule-following.

16. Only intrinsic value$_1$—ultimate value—is justifiable, and only then on an anthropocentric basis.

17. For an insightful critique of the arguments for contemporary eco-terrorism (sometimes called 'monkeywrenching'), see Turner 2006.

18. Windsor is channeling Blaise Pascal's *Pensées*: "Le cœur a ses raisons que la raison ne connaît point."

19. For Leiter, this state of affairs is surely for the worse.

20. An example might be the exemption of religious institutions from federal income tax. The exemption is unfair but should perhaps be tolerated as a means of emphasizing—fiscally and symbolically—the independence of religious institutions from state control.

21. The courts have ruled both ways in such cases: against and in favor of parents who avoid care in the name of Christian Science. See Vaughn 2013, 80–81.

22. Christian Scientists may claim that they *are* doing what is best for their children, and wilderness preservationists will claim that they *are* doing what is best for wilderness. Chapters 3 and 4 established that wilderness is not a morally considerable being, so the latter claim is inapplicable. And while I cannot disprove a religious principle asserting that it is better, in some sense, to die without the aid of modern medicine than to live with it, it is not as if Christian Science denies that health is significant aspect of a person's welfare—indeed, its commitment to spiritual healing affirms the value of life and physical well-being.

Bibliography

Abbey, Edward. 1977. *The Journey Home: Some Words in Defense of The American West*. New York: Dutton.
Aikin, Scott. 2008. "The Dogma of Environmental Revelation." *Ethics and the Environment* 13(2): 23–34.
Alvarez, Maria. 2017. "Reasons for Action: Justification, Motivation, Explanation." *The Stanford Encyclopedia of Philosophy*, edited by Edward Zalta. <https://plato.stanford.edu/archives/win2017/entries/reasons-just-vs-expl/>.
Attfield, Robin. 1981. "The Good of Trees." *The Journal of Value Inquiry* 15: 35–54.
———. 1987. *A Theory of Value and Obligation*. London: Coom Helm.
Benson, John. 2000. *Environmental Ethics: An Introduction with Readings*. London: Routledge.
Bentham, Jeremy. 1996. *An Introduction to the Principles of Morals and Legislation*. Oxford: Oxford University Press.
Birnbacher, Dieter. 2014. *Naturalness: Is the "Natural" Preferable to the "Artificial"?* Lanham, MD: University Press of America, Inc.
Breakthrough Institute. 2018. "Our Mission". Accessed September 1, 2018. https://thebreakthrough.org/about/mission/.
Brennan, Andrew, and Norva Y. S. Lo. 2021. "Environmental Ethics." *The Stanford Encyclopedia of Philosophy*, edited by Edward N. Zalta. <https://plato.stanford.edu/archives/win2021/entries/ethics-environmental/>.
Cafaro, Philip, and Sandler, Ronald, eds. 2005. *Environmental Virtue Ethics*. Lanham, MD: Rowman & Littlefield Publishers, Inc.
Callicott, J. Baird. 1998a. "The Wilderness Idea Revisited: The Sustainable Development Alternative." In *The Great New Wilderness Debate*, edited by J. Baird, Callicott and Michael Nelson, 337–66. Athens, GA: University of Georgia Press.
——— 1998b. "That Good Old-Time Wilderness Religion." In *The Great New Wilderness Debate*, edited by J. Baird Callicott and Michael Nelson, 387–95. Athens, GA: University of Georgia Press.
Callicott, J. Baird, and Nelson, Michael, eds. 1998. *The Great New Wilderness Debate*. Athens, Georgia: The University of Georgia Press.———. 2008. *The Wilderness Debate Rages On*. Athens, GA: University of Georgia Press.

Carson, Rachel. 2002. *Silent Spring*. Boston: Houghton Mifflin.
Clingerman, Forest. 2010. "Wilderness as the Place between Philosophy and Theology: Questioning Martin Drenthen on the Otherness of Nature." *Environmental Values* 19(2): 211–32.
Cockell, Charles. 2004. "The Rights of Microbes." *Interdisciplinary Science Reviews* 29(2): 141–50.
Commoner, Barry. 1971. *The Closing Circle: Nature, Man, and Technology*. New York: Knopf.
Cowen, Tyler. 2003. "Policing Nature." *Environmental Ethics* 25: 169–82.
Crist, Eileen. 2004. "Against the Social Construction of Nature and Wilderness." *Environmental Ethics* 26(1): 5–24.
Cronon, W. 1998. "The Trouble with Wilderness, or, Getting Back to the Wrong Nature." In *The Great New Wilderness Debate*, edited by J. Baird Callicott and Michael Nelson, 471-499. Athens, GA: University of Georgia Press.
Dawkins, Richard. 1995. *River Out of Eden: A Darwinian View of Life*. New York: Basic Books.
Delancey, Craig. 2012. "An Ecological Concept of Wilderness." *Ethics and the Environment* 17(1): 25–44.
Delon, Nicolas, and Purves, Duncan. 2018. "Wild Animal Suffering is Intractable." *Journal of Agricultural and Environmental Ethics* 31(2): 239–60.
DesJardins, Joseph. 2006. *Environmental Ethics: An Introduction to Environmental Philosophy*. Toronto: Thomson Wadsworth.
Dombrowski, Daniel. 2002. "Bears, Zoos, and Wilderness: The Poverty of Social Constructionism." *Society & Animals* 10(2): 195–202.
Donaldson, Sue, and Kymlicka, Will. 2014. "Animals and the Frontiers of Citizenship." *Oxford Journal of Legal Studies* 34 (2): 201–19.
Dunlap, Thomas. 2005. *Faith in Nature: Environmentalism as Religious Quest*. Seattle: University of Washington Press.
———. 2006. "Environmentalism, a Secular Faith." *Environmental Values* 15(3): 321–30.
Ellis, Erle. 2012. "The Planet of No Return: Human Resilience on an Artificial Planet." https://thebreakthrough.org/index.php/journal/past-issues/issue-2/the-planet-of-no-return.
Evernden, Neil. 1992. *The Social Creation of Nature*. Baltimore, MD: Johns Hopkins University Press.
Feinberg, Joel. 1974. "The Rights of Animals and Unborn Generations." In *Philosophy and Environmental Crisis*, edited by William Blackstone Jr., 43-68. Athens, GA: University of Georgia Press.
Foot, P. 2001. *Natural Goodness*. Oxford: Clarendon.
Friskics, Scott. 2008 "The Twofold Myth of Pristine Wilderness." *Environmental Ethics* 30(4): 381–99.
Gomez-Pompa, Arturo, and Kaus, Andrea. 1998. "Taming the Wilderness Myth." In *The Great New Wilderness Debate*, edited by J. Baird Callicott and Michael Nelson, 293-313 Athens, GA: University of Georgia Press.

Goodpaster, Kenneth. 1978. "On Being Morally Considerable." *Journal of Philosophy* 75: 308–25.

Goudarzi, Sara. 2007. "Plants Communicate to Warn Against Danger." *Live Science*. https://www.livescience.com/1909-plants-communicate-warn-danger.html.

Gould, Stephen Jay. 1982. "Nonmoral Nature." *Natural History,* February: 19–26.

Gruen, Lori. 2010. "The Moral Status of Animals." *The Stanford Encyclopedia of Philosophy*. Accessed September 1, 2018. https://plato.stanford.edu/entries/ethics-environmental/.

Guha, Ramachandra. 1998. "Radical American Environmentalism and Wilderness Preservation." In *The Great New Wilderness Debate*, edited by J. Baird Callicott and Michael Nelson, 231–45. Athens, GA: University of Georgia Press.

Hailwood, Simon. 2000. "The Value of Nature's Otherness." *Environmental Values*. 9(3): 353–72.

Hance, Jeremy. 2016. "Conservation today, the old-fashioned way." *Mongabay*, May 10. https://news.mongabay.com/2016/05/conservation-today-old-fashioned-way/.

Hargrove, Eugene. 1989. *Foundations of Environmental Ethics*. Englewood Cliffs, NJ: Prentice Hall.

Heidegger, Martin. 1949. "Letter on Humanism." http://pacificinstitute.org/pdf/Letter_on_%20Humanism.pdf .

Hill, Thomas. 1983. "Ideals of Human Excellence." *Environmental Ethics* 5: 211–24.

Horta, Oscar. 2010. "Debunking the Idyllic View of Natural Processes: Population Dynamics and Suffering in the Wild," *Télos* 17: 73–88.

———. 2017. "Animal Suffering in Nature." *Environmental Ethics*. 39(3): 261–279.

———. 2018. "Concern for wild animal suffering and environmental ethics: What are the limits of the disagreement?" *Les Ateliers de l'Éthique/The Ethics Forum*. 13(1): 85–100.

Hull, David Lee. 1982. "Philosophy and Biology." *Contemporary Philosophy: A New Survey, Philosophy of Science*, Volume 2, edited by Guttorm Floistad, 280–316. The Hague: Martinus Nijhoff.

Hume, David. 2017. *Dialogues Concerning Natural Religion*. http://www.earlymoderntexts.com/assets/pdfs/hume1779.pdf.

Hursthouse, Rosalind. 1999. *On Virtue Ethics*. Oxford: Oxford University Press.

Jamieson, Dale. 2008. *Ethics and the Environment: An Introduction*. Cambridge, UK: Cambridge University Press.

Johannsen, Kyle. 2021a. *Wild Animal Ethics: The Moral and Political Problem of Wild Animal Suffering*. New York, USA: Routledge.

———. 2021b. "Humanitarian Assistance for Wild Animals." *The Philosophers' Magazine* 93: 33–37.

Kant, Immanuel. 1994. "Critique of Judgment." In *Art and Its Significance: An Anthology of Aesthetic Theory*, edited by Stephen Ross, 93–142. Albany, NY: State University of New York Press.

Kareiva, Peter, Marvier, Michelle, and Lalasz, Robert. 2012. "Conservation in the Anthropocene: Beyond Solitude and Fragility." https://thebreakthrough.org/index.php/journal/past-issues/issue-2/conservation-in-the-anthropocene.

Kazez, Jean. 2007. *The Weight of Things: Philosophy and the Good Life*. Malden, MA: Blackwell Publishing Ltd.

Keeling, Paul. 2008. "Does the Idea of Wilderness Need a Defense?" *Environmental Values* 17(4): 505–19.

Kirchhoff, Thomas, and Vicenzotti, Vera. 2014. "A Historical and Systematic Survey of European Perceptions of Wilderness." *Environmental Values* 23(4): 443–64.

Kohák, Erazim. 1984. *The Embers and the Stars: A Philosophical Inquiry into the Moral Sense of Nature*. Chicago, IL: University of Chicago Press.

Latour, Bruno. 2012. "Love Your Monsters: Why We Must Care of Our Creations as We Do Our Children." https://thebreakthrough.org/index.php/journal/past-issues/issue-2/love-your-monsters.

Leiter, Brian. 2013. *Why Tolerate Religion?* Princeton: Princeton University Press.

Leopold, Aldo. 1991. "Some Fundamentals of Conservation in the Southwest." In *The River of the Mother of God and Other Essays*, edited by Susan Flader and J. Baird Callicott, 86–97. Madison: University of Washington Press.

———. 2002. "The Land Ethic." In *Environmental Ethics: What Really Matter, What Really Works*, edited by David Schmidtz and Elizabeth Willott, 27–32. New York: Oxford University Press, pp.

Max, D. T. 2014. "Green is Good." *The New Yorker*, May 12. https://www.newyorker.com/magazine/2014/05/12/green-is-good.

Mayr, Ernst. 1965. "Cause and effect in biology." In *Cause and Effect*, edited by in Daniel Lerner, 33–50. New York: Free Press.

McGowan, Christopher. 1997. *The Raptor and the Lamb: Predators and Prey in the Living World*. New York: Henry Holt and Company.

McKibben, Bill. 1990. *The End of Nature*. New York: Anchor Books.

McMahan, Jefferson. 2015. "The Moral Problem of Predation." In *Philosophy Comes to Dinner: Arguments About the Ethics of Eating*, edited by Andrew Chignell, Terence Cuneo, and Matt Halteman, 268–93. London: Routledge.

Mendelssohn, Moses. 1997. *Moses Mendelssohn: Philosophical Writings*. Cambridge, UK: Cambridge University Press.

Mill, John Stuart. 2000. "Nature." In *Environmental Ethics: An Introduction with Readings*, edited by John Benson, 223–36. London: Routledge.

Moore, G. E. 1922. "The Conception of Intrinsic Value." *Philosophical Studies*. London: Routledge and Kegan Paul.

Nagle, John. 2005. "The Spiritual Value of Wilderness." *Environmental Law*, Fall 35 (4): 955–59.

Nash, Roderick. 2014. *Wilderness and the American Mind*. New Haven: Yale University Press.

Nelson, Michael. 1998. "An Amalgamation of Wilderness Preservation Arguments." In *The Great New Wilderness Debate*, edited by J. Baird Callicott and Michael Nelson, 154–93. Athens, GA: University of Georgia Press.

Norcross, Alasdair. 2004. "Puppies, Pigs, and People: Eating Meat and Marginal Cases." *Philosophical Perspectives* 18 (1): 229–45.

Nordhaus, Ted, and Schellenberger, Michael. 2004. https://www.thebreakthrough.org/images/Death_of_Environmentalism.pdf.

Norton, Bryan. 1984. "Environmental Ethics and Weak Anthropocentrism." *Environmental Ethics* 6(2): 131–48.
Nozick, Robert. 2015. "The Experience Machine." In *The Ethical Life*, edited by Russ Shafer-Landau, 27–29. Oxford: Oxford University Press.
Oelschlaeger, Max. 1991. *The Idea of Wilderness: From Prehistory to the Age of Ecology*. New Haven: Yale University Press.
O'Mara, Collin. 2016. National Wildlife Federation, Fundraising Letter, May 2016.
O'Neil, John. 2003. "Metaethics." In *A Companion to Environmental Philosophy*, edited by Dale Jamieson, 163–76. Malden, MA: Blackwell.
O'Neil, John. 2008. "Wilderness, Cultivation, and Appropriation." In *The Wilderness Debate Rages On*, edited by J. Baird Callicott and Michael Nelson, 526–46. Athens, GA: University of Georgia Press.
Orr, David. 2008. "The Not-So-Great Wilderness Debate . . . Continued." In *The Wilderness Debate Rages On*, edited by J. Baird Callicott and Michael Nelson, 423–34. Athens, GA: University of Georgia Press.
Otto, Rudolf. 1958. *The Idea of the Holy: An Inquiry into the non-rational factor in the idea of the divine and its relation to the rational*. London: Oxford University Press.
Palmer, Clare. 2018. "Should we help wild animals suffering negative impacts from climate change?" In *Professionals in Food Chains*, edited by Svenja Springer and Herwig Grimm, 35–40. The Netherlands: Wageningen Academic Publishers.
Passmore, John. 1974. *Man's Responsibility for Nature: Ecological Problems and Western Traditions*. New York: Scribner.
Pearce, David. 2015. "A Welfare State for Elephants? A Case Study of Compassionate Stewardship." *Relations. Beyond Anthropocentrism* 3(2): 153–64.
Pittendrigh, Colin. 1958. "Adaptation, natural selection, and behavior." In *Behavior and Evolution*, edited by Anne Roe and Gaylord Simpson, 390–416. New Haven: Yale University Press.
Rawls, John. 1993. *Political Liberalism*. New York, NY: Columbia University Press.
———. 1997. "The Idea of Public Reason Revisited." *University of Chicago Law Review* 64: 765–807.
Regan, Tom. 1983. *The Case for Animal Rights*. Berkeley: University of California Press.
Reese, J. 2015. "Wild animals endure illness, injury, and starvation. We should help." Vox, December 14. http://www.vox.com/2015/12/14/9873012/wild-animals-suffering.
Rolston, Holmes. 1998. "The Wilderness Idea Reaffirmed." In *The Great New Wilderness Debate*, edited by J. Baird Callicott and Michael Nelson, 367–86. Athens, GA: University of Georgia.
———. 2002. "Values in and Duties to the Natural World." In *Environmental Ethics: What Really Matter, What Really Works*, edited by David Schmidtz and Elizabeth Willott, 33-38. New York: Oxford University Press.
Routley, Richard. 1973. "Is There a Need for a New, an Environmental Ethic?" https://iseethics.files.wordpress.com/2013/02/routley-richard-is-there-a-need-for-a-new-an-environmental-ethic-original.pdf.

Routley, Richard. and Routley, Val. 1980. "Human Chauvanism and Environmental Ethics." In *Environmental Philosophy*, edited by Mannison, McRobbie, and Routley, R., 96–189. Canberra: Research School of Social Sciences, Australian National University.

Sagoff, Mark. 1984. "Animal Liberation and Environmental Ethics: Bad Marriage, Quick Divorce." *Osgoode Hall Law Journal* 22(2): 297–307.

———. 2015. "A Theology for Ecomodernism: What is the Nature we Seek to Save?" https://thebreakthrough.org/index.php/journal/past-issues/issue-5/a-theology-for-ecomodernism.

Sandel, Michael. 2007. *The Case against Perfection: Ethics in the Age of Genetic Engineering*. Cambridge, MA: Belknap of Harvard University Press.

Sandler, Ronald. 2007. *Character and Environment: A Virtue-Oriented Approach to Environmental Ethics*. New York: Columbia University Press.

Savulescu, Julian. 2007. "Genetic Intervention and the Ethics of Enhancement of Human Beings." In *The Oxford Handbook of Bioethics*, edited by Bonnie Steinbock, 516–35. Oxford University Press.

Schopenhauer, Arthur. 1970. *Essays and Aphorisms*. London: Penguin.

Singer, Peter. 1990. *Animal Liberation: A New Ethics for our Treatment of Animals*. New York: Avon Books.

Snyder, Gary. 2008. "Is Nature Real?" In *The Wilderness Debate Rages On*, edited by J. Baird Callicott and Michael Nelson, 352–54. Athens, GA: University of Georgia Press.

Taylor, Paul. "The Ethics of Respect for Nature." In *The Ethical Life*, edited by Russ Shafer-Landau, 319–31. Oxford: Oxford University Press.

Thompson, Jana. 1990. "A Refutation of Environmental Ethics." *Environmental Ethics* 12(2): 147–60.

Turner, Derek. 2005. "Are We at War With Nature?" *Environmental Values* 14: 21–36.

———. 2006. "Monkeywrenching, Perverse Incentives, and Ecodefence." *Environmental Values* 15: 213–32.

Unger, Peter. 1996. *Living High & Letting Die: Our Illusion of Innocence*. Oxford: Oxford University Press.

Varner, Gary. 1998. *In Nature's Interests? Interests, Animal Rights, and Environmental Ethics*. New York: Oxford University Press.

Vaughn, Lewis. 2013. *Bioethics: Principles, Issues, and Cases*. New York: Oxford University Press.

Vogel, Steven. 2002. "Environmental Philosophy After the End of Nature". *Environmental Ethics* 24(1): 23–29.

Weston, Anthony. 1985. "Beyond Intrinsic Value." *Environmental Ethics* 7(4): 321–39.

Wilcox, Christine. 2011. "Bambi or Bessie: Are wild animals happier?" Ecology.com, October 20. http://www.ecology.com/2011/10/20/bambi-bessie-wild-animals-happier/.

Wilderness Act. 1964. Public Law 88–577 (16 U.S. C. 1131-1136) 88th Congress, Second Session, September 3. https://www.wilderness.net/NWPS/documents/publiclaws/PDF/16_USC_1131-1136.pdf.

Williams, Bernard. 1985. *Making Sense of Humanity and Other Philosophical Papers, 1982–1983*. Cambridge: Cambridge University Press, 1995.

———. 1994. "Must a Concern for the Environment Be Centered on Human Beings?" In *Reflecting on Nature: Readings in Environmental Philosophy*, edited by Lori Gruen and Dale Jamieson, 46–52. New York: Oxford University Press.

Williams, George Christopher. 1966. Adaptation and Natural Selection: A Critique of Some Current Evolutionary Thought. Princeton, NJ: Princeton University Press.

Windsor, Charles. 2002. "A Reflection on the 2000 Reith Lectures." BBC Radio 4, May 17. https://www.princeofwales.gov.uk/media/speeches/speech-hrh-the-prince-of-wales-titled-reflection-the-2000-reith-lectures-bbc-radio-4.

Woods, Mark. 2017. *Rethinking Wilderness*. Peterborough, Ontario, Canada: Broadview Press.

Index

Abbey, Edward, ix, 87, 111–12, 124n5
aboriginal peoples, 7–9
AFW. *See* Argument from Welfare
Aiken, Scott, 114
appeal to nature, xi, 68
Anderson, Clinton, 113
animal rights, 19, 41n3, 53
animals: carnivorous, as a moral problem, 19, 35; domesticated vs. wild, 32; humans in relation to, 11–12, 36; moral considerability of, 27–28, 36–39, 42n4; suffering experienced by, in the wild, xii, 23, 26–28, 30–34, 36. *See also* animal welfare; nonhuman natural world
animal welfare: approaches to, 41n3; environmentalists' conventional position on, xii; wilderness preservation beneficial to, xii, 24–29; wilderness preservation harmful to, xii, 23–24, 33–39. *See also* Argument from Welfare; Objection from Welfare
Anthropocene, 90–92
anthropocentrism: considered less moral than nonanthropocentrism, 25–26, 46–48; features of, 51; nonanthropocentrism in conflict with, 51; and responsibility, 109; strong vs. weak, 71n1; theocentrism in relation to, 72n4; wilderness preservation arguments based on, 25–26, 76, 81–84. *See also* nonanthropocentrism
argument from design, 93n5
Argument from Welfare (AFW), 24–29, 39, 80
Aristotelianism, 63, 65, 68
art gallery argument, 83
artificial worlds: as corrective for the suffering in nature, 31; plausibility of, xiii, 76, 89; substitutability of, for wilderness, 39, 57, 85–87, 92–93, 97–98
Attfield, Robin, 53–54, 62–63

Benson, John, 47
Bentham, Jeremy, 27, 42n4, 51, 52
biocentrism, xii–xiii, 42n4, 53–54, 61–66
bioethics, xiii, 98–104
Breakthrough Institute, xiii, 76, 89–92, 100, 121
Brennan, Andrew, 51
Burroughs, John, 112

Callicott, J. Baird, 7–8, 10–13, 17–18, 20n3, 125n11
carnivores, as a moral problem, 19, 35

Carson, Rachel, *Silent Spring*, 51, 81
cathedral argument, 124n10
Christian Coalition, 115
Christian Science, 122, 126n22
Clingerman, Forrest, 112
Commoner, Barry, 42n7
conservationism, 24–26
Crist, Eileen, 15
Cronon, William, 7–8, 10, 12, 14–15
cultural objections to wilderness idea, 6–10
Cupitt, Don, 15

Darwin, Charles, 30–31
Dawkins, Richard, 31, 36–38
DeLancey, Craig, 3
Derrida, Jacques, 15
DesJardins, Joseph, 55, 67–68
Dillon, Tom, 26
Dombrowski, Daniel, 16
Dunlap, Thomas, 114, 120

ecocentrism, xii–xiii, 42n4, 54–56, 66–69, 74n20
ecological holism, 12
eco-terrorists and eco-terrorism, 120, 126n17
Ellis, Erle, 91–92
Emerson, Ralph Waldo, 18
enlightened self-interest, 81
Enlightenment, 10, 89–90
environmental ethics: bioethics compared to, xiii, 98–103; conventional position of, on nonhuman natural world, x; ecocentrism conflated with, 74n20; human/nature divide fundamental to, 14; and the idea of wilderness, 1–2, 4–5; infancy of, 40–41; and intrinsic value of nature, 46–48; moral problems confronting, xii; nonanthropocentric positions favored in, xii, 41, 46–48, 51–52, 76–77. *See also* environmentalism

environmentalism: American, 6, 8; Arguments from Welfare in, 24–26; conservationism vs. preservationism in, 24–26, 40; critiques of, 89; and the idea of wilderness, 17–19; moral grandstanding in, 40–41; opposition to Objections from Welfare in, 33–39; religiosity linked to, 114; and wilderness preservation, xii, 8, 17–19. *See also* environmental ethics
Epictetus, 104
ethical holism, 55
ethnic objections to wilderness idea, 6–10
ethnocentrism, 6–7
Evernden, Neil, 15
experience machine, 86–87, 95n15

Falkowski, Paul, 42n8
Feinberg, Joel, 52–53
First Amendment, 121
Foot, Philippa, 66
freedom, 105–6, 108, 123n5, 124n8
Friskics, Scott, 5–6, 113

Gaia hypothesis, 71, 78–80, 93n5
germline genetic modification, 19, 35, 36
giftedness of life: mastery and enhancement of nature antithetical to, xiii, 98, 102–6; moral values fostered by, 104–11; spiritual/religious associations of, 115–16; wilderness compared to, xiii, 106–11
global justice, 109
Gomez-Pompa, Arturo, 7–9
Goodpaster, Kenneth, 42n4, 53–54, 61–63, 64
Gore, Al, *An Inconvenient Truth*, 51, 81
Gospels, 9
Greenpeace, 28
Guha, Ramachandra, 6, 7, 8, 18, 20n1, 21n7

Habermas, Jürgen, 105, 108, 124n8

Hailwood, Simon, 20n5
Hance, Jeremy, 25–26
Hargrove, Eugene, 31, 42n7, 99–100
Hegel, G. W. F., 118, 125n13
Heidegger, Martin, 21n8
Hull, David, 65–66
humans: animals in relation to, 11–12, 36; augmentation of nature by, xii, xiv, 35–36, 45, 76, 89, 92, 97; domain of the other-than-human vs., xiv, 20n5, 76, 87–88, 93, 95n15, 111–15, 118, 124n10; mastery and enhancement of nature by, 98, 100–106; nature in relation to, 10–12, 14, 20n5, 101–6
Hume, David, 93n5
humility, 104–8
Humphrey, Hubert, 113
Hursthouse, Rosalind, 66, 74n17

instrumental value, xiii, 48, 81–84
interests, beings with, 42, 51–54, 62–65, 72n7
intrinsic value: critiques of appeals to, 56–61, 80; environmental ethics and, 46–48; independent of valuers, 50, 58–61; as morally considerable, 49; as non-relational, 50, 57–58; types of, 48–50; as ultimate/non-instrumental, 48–49; of wilderness, x, xii, 47–48, 56–61, 77, 80
isolation tests, 57–60
is-ought problem, 68

James, William, 114
Jamieson, Dale, 5, 42n4, 47, 49, 54, 60–61, 64–66, 72n3, 88, 110

Kant, Immanuel, 95n15, 110
Kareiva, Peter, 90–91, 96n17
Kaus, Andrea, 7–9
Kearns, Laurel, 114–15
Keeling, Paul, 4–5, 10, 12–13
Kierkegaard, Søren, 118–19, 121, 125n15

Kohak, Erazim, 47

Lalasz, Robert, 90–91, 96n17
land ethic, 55–56
land health, 18
Larrere, Catherine, 15
last man scenarios, 58–60
Latour, Bruno, 89–90, 101
League of Conservation Voters, 115
Leiter, Brian, 122, 126n19
Leopold, Aldo, 18, 55–56, 66–67, 69, 70, 99
life-support argument, 93n2
Lo, Norva, 51
Lyell, Charles, 30

marginal cases, 73–74n16
Marvier, Michelle, 90–91, 96n17
Marx, Karl, and Marxism, 19, 21n8
May, William F., 115
Mayr, Ernest, 65
McKibben, Bill, 5, 87–88, 111–13, 115
McMahan, Jefferson, 19, 29, 34–35, 38–40, 42n8
Mendelssohn, Moses, 95n15
mental therapy argument, 83–84
Mill, J. S., 4, 12, 52, 68
Mongabay (news web site), 25
Moore, G. E, 50, 57, 58
morality: animals as subjects for, 27–28, 36–39, 41n3; anthropocentrism vs. nonanthropocentrism as basis for, 51–52; biocentrism as basis for, 53–54, 61–66; carnivores as problem for, 19, 35; duties of beneficence vs. duties of non-maleficence in, 38–40; ecocentrism as basis for, 54–56, 66–69; environmental ethics and problems of, xii, 40–41; expansion of, beyond anthropocentrism, 36–37, 61–69; Gaia hypothesis and, 78–80; giftedness of life as component of, 103–11; intrinsic value associated with, 49; nature lacking in, 68; nonanthropocentrism

considered more aligned with, than anthropocentrism, 25–26, 39; nonsentient plants and animals as subjects for, 42n4; religious considerations compared to those of, xiv, 99, 117–23; responsibility attached to, 104–6, 109–11; sentientism as basis for, 52–53, 64–65; wilderness lacking in, 109–10; wilderness preservation and problems of, xii, xiii, 23–41
Muir, John, 18, 24–25, 124n10

Naess, Arne, 74n20
Nagle, John, 20n5, 113
Nash, Roderick, 6, 87
National Wildlife Federation, 28–29
natural resources argument, 82–83
nature: amoral character of, 68; defined, 4; humans in relation to, 10–12, 14, 20n5, 101–6; mastery and enhancement of, 98, 100–106; social constructivist objection to idea of, 14–17. *See also* nonhuman natural world; wilderness
Nel, Deon, 26
Nelson, Michael, 24, 77–78, 81, 83–84, 86, 94n8, 94n12, 121, 123n5, 124n10
new conservationism, 25–26
nonanthropocentrism: AFW grounded in, 25, 39; anthropocentrism in conflict with, 51; considered more moral than anthropocentrism, 25–26, 39; critiques of, 61–69; in environmental ethics, xii, 41, 46–48, 51–52, 76–77; types of, 52–56; value based in, x, xii, 47, 51–52; wilderness preservation arguments based on, x, xii–xiii, 25, 45–71, 76–80
nonhuman natural world: extension of morality to, 42n4; value of, x, 24. *See also* animals; nature; wilderness
nonsentient beings, 42n4
Nordhaus, Ted, 89

Norton, Bryan, 47, 71n1
Nozick, Robert, 86–87, 93, 95n15

Objection from Welfare (OFW): human augmentation of wilderness based on, xii, xiv, 97, 110–11; overview of, 29–33; points of agreement with AFW, 29, 80; practicability of acting on, 34–36, 40; rebuttals to and defenses of, xii, xiii, 33–39, 45–46, 61, 70, 106, 110–11; spiritual/religious value and, 117–23
Oelschlaeger, Max, 1
OFW. *See* Objection from Welfare (OFW)
Olson, Sigurd, 113
O'Neill, John, 15–16, 50
Orr, David, 16, 17, 19
Otto, Rudolph, 112
Ouspensky, Pyotr, 55–56

parasitism, 32
Passmore, John, 10
performance enhancing drugs (PEDs), 102–3
philosophy: critique of analytic, 95n16; environmentalists' objection to, 17–19; objection to wilderness idea from standpoint of, 10–14
Pinchot, Gifford, 18, 24–25
Plato, 89
postmodernism, 15
precautionary principle, 94n8, 110
predation, 31, 34–35
preservationism, 24–26
Promethean aspirations, xiii, 98, 100–106
public reason, 119, 121, 125n14

racial objections to wilderness idea, 6–10
Rawls, John, 121, 125n14
realism, 72n3
received wilderness idea, 2–3, 5–6, 10, 17–18, 20n3, 125n11

Regan, Tom, 41n3, 47, 52–53, 65, 67, 69
responsibility, moral, 104–6, 109–11
Rolston, Holmes, III, 8, 11–12, 16–17, 56, 66, 71, 74n20, 125n11
Routley, Richard, 46–47, 51, 58–60, 73n11, 73n12
Routley, Val, 58–60, 73n11, 73n12
Rush, A. J., 113
Rutherford, Ernest, 35

Sagoff, Mark, 19–20, 29–30, 32–33, 114
Salaman, Paul, 26
Sandel, Michael, xiii, 98, 101–10, 115–17, 123n3, 123n5, 124n6, 124n8, 125n12
Savulescu, Julian, 124n6
Schellenberger, Michael, 89
Schopenhauer, Arthur, 30
science: advances and promises of, 35, 89–90, 92, 99–100; defense of, 9–10; skepticism about, 7, 9
sentientism: AFW and, 26–28; biocentrism vs., 53–54, 64–65; moral considerability based on, 52–53, 64–65; moral responsibility associated with, 109; OFW and, 29–33; overview of, 52–53; viability of, 70; wilderness preservation grounded in, xii–xiii. *See also* suffering
Shelley, Mary, *Frankenstein*, 89–90, 100–101
Singer, Peter, 27, 40, 41n3, 42n4, 52–53
Snyder, Gary, 10, 13, 17, 100
social bonding argument, 82–83
social constructivism, 14–17
solidarity, 105–8
Soule, Michael, 25
speciesism, 27–28
spiritual/religious values: as non-ethical consideration for wilderness preservation, xiv, 99, 117–23; OFW and, 117–23; opposition of, to science, 10; role of, in secular society, xiv, 121; wilderness preservation based on, xiv, 69, 99, 111–23; wilderness *qua* wilderness as, xiv, 98–99, 111–16, 125n11
stewardship, 24
Stoics, 68, 104
stress, 32
sublime, 95n15
suffering: beneficial/just/chosen vs. their opposites, 29–30, 32–33, 38–39; measures for alleviating, 33; moral considerability predicated on capacity for, 27–28, 38–39, 41n3; as moral problem, 36–37; in the wild, xii, 23, 30–34, 36. *See also* sentientism

Tansley, Arthur, 67
Taylor, Paul, 53–54, 62–63, 70, 72n7
technology, care of, 89–90
teleology, 62–65
teleonomy, 65–66
theocentrism, 72n4
therapeutic nihilism, 42n7, 99–100, 110
Thompson, Jana, 42n4, 69, 98
Thoreau, Henry David, 18
thought experiments, about wilderness, xi–xii, xiii, 76, 85–89

ultimate value, xiii, 48–49, 81–84
utilitarianism, 51, 52

Varner, Gary, 62
virtue ethics, 59, 73n12, 174n17, 120
Vogel, Steven, 11–13

Weston, Anthony, 47
Wilcox, Christie, 32
wilderness: amoral character of, 109–10; anthropocentric value of, xii, xiii; cultural/ethnic/racial objection to idea of, 6–10; defined, 1–3; degrees of, 5; empirical objection to idea of, 4–6; environmental objection to idea of, 17–19; freedom associated

with, 124n5; giftedness compared to, xiii, 106–11; human augmentation of, xii, xiv, 35–36, 45, 76, 89, 92, 97; idea of, xii, 1–20; intrinsic value of, x, xii, 47–48, 56–61, 77, 80; nature contrasted with, 4; as other-than-human, xiv, 20n5, 76, 87–88, 93, 95n15, 111–15, 118, 124n10; philosophical objection to idea of, 10–14; philosophical questions concerning, ix; received idea of, 2–3, 5–6, 10, 17–18, 20n3, 125n11; relational values of, 75; social constructivist objection to idea of, 14–17; spiritual/religious value of, xiv, 98–99, 111–16, 125n11; suffering experienced by creatures in, xii, 23, 30–34, 36; as sufficient but not necessary source, 84–85. *See also* nature; wilderness *qua* wilderness

Wilderness Act (1964), xii, 1–5, 20n5, 75, 113–14

wilderness preservation: animal welfare arguments against, xii, 23–24, 33–39, 97; animal welfare arguments for, xii, 24–29; anthropocentric arguments for, 25–26, 76, 81–84, 106–11; environmentalists' approach to, xii, 8, 17–19; as human choice, ix; instrumental-value arguments for, 82–84; as moral problem, xii, xiii, 23–41, 120–23; moral responsibility and, 109–11; nonanthropocentric arguments for/against, x, xii–xiii, 25–26, 45–71, 76–80 (*see also* value of wilderness *qua* wilderness as argument for); spiritual/religious argument for, xiv, 69, 99, 111–23; thought experiments about, x–xi, xiii, 76, 85–89; ultimate-value arguments for, 82–84; value of wilderness *qua* wilderness as argument for, xiii–xiv, 97–98, 101

wilderness *qua* wilderness: defined, xivn1, 75; giftedness not equivalent to, 106–8; as spiritual/religious value, xiv, 98–99, 111–16; the sublime compared to, 95n15; thought experiments about, 88–89; value of, xiii, xivn1, 57, 75, 76, 84–88, 92–93 (*see also* as spiritual/religious value)

wildlife. *See* animals

Williams, Bernard, 42n4, 65, 68–69, 101

Wilson, E. O., 25

Windsor, Charles, Prince of Wales, 120–21, 123n2

Wittgenstein, Ludwig, 12–13

Woods, Mark, 20n2

world-X, 85–87, 92, 98

About the Author

Joshua S. Duclos holds a PhD in philosophy from Boston University. He teaches philosophy and humanities at St. Paul's School in Concord, New Hampshire.

www.ingramcontent.com/pod-product-compliance
Lightning Source LLC
Chambersburg PA
CBHW020126010526
44115CB00008B/987